LIFELINES

ELEMENTARY STUDENT'S BOOK

TOM HUTCHINSON

OXFORD UNIVERSITY PRESS

Contents

Contents

Contents

1 Getting started

Hello

1 Look at the picture.

Hello, I'm Enrique.

Pleased to meet you, Enrique. My name's Lyn.

a 📼 *1.1* Listen and repeat the conversation.

b Practise the conversation with a partner. Use your own names.

Enrique Hello, I'm Enrique.
Lyn Pleased to meet you, Enrique. My name's Lyn.
Enrique Nice to meet you, Lyn.
Lyn Where are you from?
Enrique I'm from Spain. And you?
Lyn I'm from London.

Vocabulary file: Countries

a Match the flags and countries.

France	Switzerland	Italy
Brazil	Argentina	Spain
the USA	Poland	Turkey
Hungary	Japan	the UK

1 _____
2 _____
3 _____
4 _____
5 _____
6 _____
7 _____
8 _____
9 _____
10 _____
11 _____
12 _____

b 📼 *1.2* Listen, check, and repeat.

c What's the capital of each country?

EXAMPLE
The capital of Argentina is Buenos Aires.

2 Look at the people.

Banu

Fernando and Telma

Sarah and Michael

Gábor

Paolo

Keiko

a 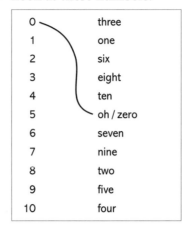 *1.3* Listen and complete the conversation.

A Hi. I'm _____ .

B Nice _____ meet you, _____ . My name's _____ .

A Pleased to _____ you, _____ . Where are _____ from?

B I'm from _____ . And you?

A I'm from _____ .

b 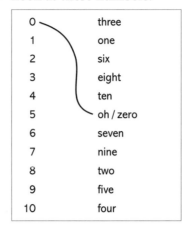 *1.3* Listen again and check.

c Go round the class and introduce yourself.

3 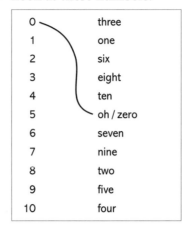 *1.4* **Listen to some more conversations.**

a Where are the people from?

b Work with a partner. Practise introducing the people in the pictures.

EXAMPLES

This is _____ . He's / She's from _____ .

This is _____ and _____ . They're from _____ .

4 **Introduce your partner to the class.**

Numbers

1 **Look at these numbers.**

0	three
1	one
2	six
3	eight
4	ten
5	oh / zero
6	seven
7	nine
8	two
9	five
10	four

a Match the numbers and words.

b 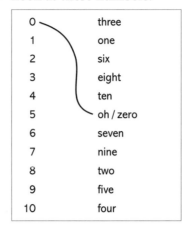 *1.5* Listen, check, and repeat.

2 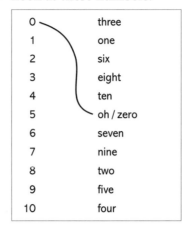 *1.6* **Listen to the four telephone numbers.**

a Write down the numbers.

b Ask people in the class *What's your phone number?*

3 **Look at these numbers.**

a What are the missing numbers?

11	eleven	21	twenty-one
12	twelve	22	_____
13	thirteen	30	_____
14	_____	40	forty
15	fifteen	50	_____
16	_____	60	sixty
17	seventeen	70	_____
18	_____	80	eighty
19	nineteen	90	_____
20	_____	100	a hundred / one hundred

b Check your ideas in the **Wordlist** on p115.

4 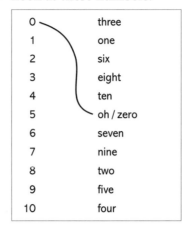 *1.7* **Listen. Which of these numbers do you hear?**

75	61	42	79	15
16	18	60	53	80

Classroom language (1)

1 📼 *1.8* **Listen and repeat the alphabet.**

a b c d e f g h i j k l m
n o p q r s t u v w x y z

2 Look at the classroom.

a Label the things in the picture. Use a dictionary to help you.

b 📼 *1.9* Listen and check. Practise saying the words with a partner.

3 Look at the words.

a What is the rule for using *a* or *an*?

b Ask and answer about the picture with a partner.

EXAMPLE
A What's this called in English?
B It's an umbrella.
A How do you spell that?
B It's U-M-B-R-E-double L-A.

➤ Check the rules for *a* / *an* in **Grammar Reference 1.1**.

4 Here are some useful expressions.

1 **A** What does *window* mean?
 B It means *ventana*.

2 **A** How do you say *au revoir* in English?
 B It's *goodbye*.

3 **A** How do you spell *door*?
 B It's D-double O-R.

4 **A** Can you repeat that, please?
 B Yes, of course, D-double O-R.

5 **A** Turn to p19.
 B I'm sorry, I don't understand.

6 **A** How do you pronounce this word?
 B I don't know.

a 📼 *1.10* Listen and repeat.

b Use the expressions. Ask your teacher or your partner about some more things in the picture or in your class.

➤ See **Functional Language: Useful expressions** p112.

Personal information

1  *1.11* **Listen to the conversation.**

a Complete the card.

b Complete these questions from the conversation.

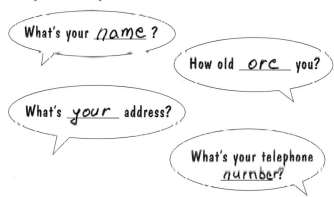

c *1.11* Listen again and check.

2 **Work with a partner. Ask the questions and complete the card for your partner.**

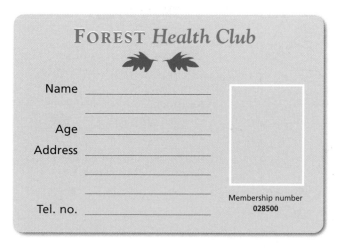

Plurals

1 **Look at the words.**

a How do we make plurals?

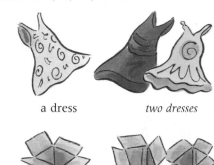

a book   *two books*

b What happens to the plural when the word ends in *-s, -x, -sh,* or *-ch*?

a dress   *two dresses*

a box   *two boxes*

a toothbrush   *two toothbrushes*

a watch   *two watches*

c  *1.12* Listen, check, and repeat.

➤ See **Pronunciation: *-es* endings** p25.

2 **Some plurals are irregular.**

EXAMPLES
a man *two men*   a woman *three women*
a child *ten children*   a person *five people*

a *1.13* Listen and repeat.

b Look at the picture on p8. What plural things can you see?

EXAMPLE
three students

➤ Check the rules for plurals in **Grammar Reference 1.3**.

Adjectives

1 Look at these adjectives.

a Write them under the correct pictures. Use a dictionary to help you.

| fat | old | big | new | expensive | tall | bad | fast | thin | light |

1 _____ young

2 _____ slow

3 heavy _____

4 old _____

5 _____ cheap

6 thick _____

7 _____ short

8 good _____

9 _____ slim

10 _____ small

b Check your ideas with a partner.

2 Put the words in the correct order.

EXAMPLE

old an man   _an old man_

cars two fast   _____

shoes new   _____

small dog a   _____

3 Look at the names of the colours.

pink orange blue grey yellow green brown white red purple black

a Work with a partner. Point to things in your class or in the book and ask questions.

EXAMPLE
A What colour is that?
B It's red and white.

b 🔲 _1.14_ Look at exercise 1. Listen. Are the statements _True_ (✓) or _False_ (✗)?

EXAMPLE
The fast car is red. ✗
The fast car is green.

➤ Check the rules for adjectives in **Grammar Reference 1.4**.

In a café

1 Look at the menu.

a 🖭 *1.15* Listen to the conversations. What do the people buy?

b 🖭 *1.15* Listen again and complete the conversations.

1 **Assistant** _____ , please?
Customer Two _____ , please.
Assistant Anything else?
Customer No, _____ you.
Assistant That's £5.20, _____ .
Customer Thank you.

2 **Assistant** Yes, please?
Customer A _____ and a _____ , please.
Assistant Small or large?
Customer _____ , please.
Assistant That's £ _____ , please.
Customer Thank you.

3 **Assistant** Yes, please?
Customer A _____ coffee, please.
Assistant Anything else?
Customer No, _____ .
Assistant _____ p, please.
Customer Thank you.

Language focus: Saying prices

a Look at these prices.
£3.20   *three pounds twenty*
50p   *fifty pence* or *fifty p*

b Say these prices.

£1.20	64p	£9.45	12p
75p	£9	£1.15	99p

c 🖭 *1.16* Listen, check, and repeat.

2 Work with a partner.

a Practise the conversations.

b Look at the menu. Make new conversations.

2 People

Grammar
The verb *to be*

Grammar in use

1 📼 *2.1* **Read and listen to the conversations.**

2 **Answer these questions.**
1 Where is the meeting?
2 Where is Ms Watson?
3 Where are Mr and Mrs Smith from?

1

*Excuse me.
Are you Ms Watson?*

*No, I'm not.
She's over there.*

Thank you.

2

*Are Mr and Mrs Smith
from America?*

*No, they aren't.
They're from Canada.*

3

*Excuse me. Is the
meeting here?*

*No, it isn't.
It's in room 10.*

Rules

1 Look at the table.

a Add the short forms of the verb *to be*.

're	's	'm

	am ____	here.
I	am not ____	
He	is ____	
She		from Portugal.
It	is not ____	
We	are ____	in room ten.
You		
They	are not ____	

b Find the negative short forms in the conversations. Add them to the table.

2 How do we make questions with the verb *to be*?

The meeting is here.

_____ here?

They are from America.

_____ from America?

3 Look at the conversations again.

a Complete the short answers.

1 **A** Are you Ms Watson?
  B No, I'm _____ .

2 **A** Are Mr and Mrs Smith from America?
  B No, they _____ .

3 **A** Is the meeting here?
  B No, it _____ .

b Give the short answers for these conversations.

Practice

1 Complete the conversations with the correct form of the verb *to be*.

1 **A** _____ this your pen?
  B No, it _____ .

2 **A** _____ you from Spain?
  B No, I _____ . I _____ from Argentina.

3 **A** Where _____ the meeting?
  B It _____ in the room over there.

4 **A** Mr and Mrs James _____ here.
  B Where _____ they?
  A They _____ on holiday.

5 **A** Excuse me. _____ you Mr and Mrs Wilson?
  B No, we _____ . We _____ Mr and Mrs Smith.

2 Work with a partner. Ask and answer about the people in your class or on page 7.

EXAMPLES

A *Is _____ from Brazil?*
B *Yes, he / she is / No, he / she isn't. He / she's from _____ .*
A *Are _____ from Turkey?*
B *Yes, they are / No, they aren't. They're from _____ .*

3 Write true sentences.

1 We _____ in room 10.
2 I _____ from Canada.
3 My name _____ .
4 My partner _____ from Britain.
5 We _____ in a meeting.
6 My favourite colours _____ .
7 I _____ tall.
8 New York _____ .
9 _____ my favourite city.
10 Our teacher _____ .

A Are you Ms Watson?
B Yes, I _____ .

A Are Mr and Mrs Smith from Canada?
B Yes, _____ _____ .

A Is the meeting here?
B Yes, _____ _____ .

➤ Check the rules for the verb *to be* in **Grammar Reference 2.1**.

Vocabulary
Classroom language (2)

1 Look at these instructions.

Stand up.

Sit down.

Pick up your pen.

Put down your pen.

Open your book.

Close your book.

Come here.

Go to the board.

Listen.

Read.

Write.

Say *Hello*.

Hello.

Turn to page 5.

Page 5.

Look at exercise 3.

Exercise 3.

Look.

Don't look.

2 2.2 Listen and follow the instructions.

3 Work with a partner. Give him / her some instructions.

Reading and writing
People and jobs

1 2.3 Read and listen to the texts.

a

I'm Walter Bergen and I'm from New York in the USA. I'm thirty-one years old and I'm a doctor. I'm married. My wife's name is Candy and she's an architect. She's thirty-one, too. In this photo we're on holiday in Florida.

b

My name's Meena Kuhmar. I'm twenty-six years old and I'm from Bristol in England, but my parents are from India. I'm a dentist and I'm married. My husband is twenty-seven and he's an engineer. His name's Suresh. In this photo we're in our garden.

c

My name's Tim Caldwell. I'm from Melbourne in Australia. I'm twenty years old and I'm a student. I'm not married. My girlfriend is a secretary. Her name's Glenda and she's twenty-two. In this photo we're with her parents at their house.

2 **Match the texts and the pictures.**
1 Who are the people in each picture?
2 Where are they?

3 **Complete the sentences with *his, her, he's,* or *she's.***
1 This is my wife. _____ name's Maria. _____ a doctor and _____ twenty-nine years old.
2 My boyfriend's a waiter. _____ name's Sven. In this photo _____ in London with _____ parents.
3 This is Alan with _____ girlfriend. _____ a teacher. _____ name's Annette and _____ from Belgium.
4 Suzie is a hairdresser. _____ married. _____ husband is a shop assistant. _____ name's Joe.

4 **Look at the texts again. Glenda, Suresh, and Candy are introducing themselves and their partners. Write their texts.**

5 **Write a paragraph about yourself. Add a photograph.**

My name's _____ . I'm from _____ in _____ .
I'm _____ years old and I'm a / an _____ .
I'm (not) married. My wife / husband / girlfriend / boyfriend is _____ . His / her name's _____ .
He / she's _____ years old. In this photo we're _____ .

Language focus: Possessive adjectives

a Look at the texts again and complete the table.

subject pronoun	possessive adjective
I	_____
he	_____
she	_____
it	its
we	_____
you	your
they	_____

b Look at these sentences.
His name's Tim.   *Her name's Glenda.*

c When do we use *his* or *her*? Is it the same in your language?

➤ Check the rules for possessive adjectives in **Grammar Reference 2.4**.

Vocabulary file: Jobs

a Complete the names of these jobs. Use a dictionary to help you.

ctu_____	sec_____
waiter / waitress	arch_____
shop assistant	den_____
do_____	eng_____
tea_____	nurse
bank clerk	pil_____

b 🔊 *2.4* Listen, check, and repeat.

c Look at these sentences. Compare them with your language.
I'm a dentist.
She's an architect.

d Work with a partner. Ask and answer about the people in the pictures.
EXAMPLE
A *Is Suresh a bank clerk?*
B *No, he isn't. He's an engineer.*

e Ask people in your class about their jobs.
EXAMPLE
A *What do you do?*
   (or *What do you want to be?*)
B *I'm a hairdresser.*
   (or *I want to be a hairdresser.*)

Listening and speaking
Meeting people

1 Look at the pictures.

a  2.5 Listen to the conversations.

b Label these people.

| Ken | Melanie | Barry | Maria | Jason |

a *Melanie*

b *Jason*

c *Barry*

d *Ken*

e *Maria*

2 **Listen again and answer these questions.**
1 Where is Ken from?
2 What is his job?
3 What is Maria's job?
4 Is Melanie a doctor?
5 Are Ken and Maria married?
6 How does Melanie feel?

3 **Complete the paragraph about Ken.**

Ken is an _____ . He's from _____
in _____ . He's _____ . His wife
_____ . Her name _____ .

Conversation pieces: Meeting people

a Complete the conversations.

| Pleased | from | a | do | about |
| interesting | How | are | I'm | an |

1 A Hello, _I'm_ Barry.
  B _How_ do you do, Barry? I'm Maria.
  A _please_ to meet you. What _do_ you do?
  B I'm _a_ nurse.
  A That's _interesting_
  B What _about_ you?
  A I'm _an_ engineer.
  B Where _are_ you from?
  A I'm _from_ Canada.

| all | you | bye | be | fine | Hi |
| are | See | How |

2 A _Hi_ . How _are_ you?
  B I'm _fine_ , thanks. And _you_ ?
  A Oh, not bad. _How_ are the kids?
  B They're _all_ fine.
  A Well, I must _be_ off. _See_ you.
  B Yes, _bye_ .

b 2.6 Listen and check.

c Practise the conversations with a partner.

---

4 **You're at a party.**

a Go round and meet new people. Use conversation **1** above. (You can invent a job!)

b Go round again. This time use conversation **2** to talk to your friends.

➤ See **Functional Language: Meeting people** p112.

Pronunciation
The IPA; word stress

1 The IPA (the phonetic alphabet)

English spelling and pronunciation are often not the same. The International Phonetic Alphabet (IPA) shows you how a word is pronounced.

a Look at these words and sounds.

same spelling	different sound
house	/aʊ/
your	/ɔ:/

different spelling	same sound
what	/ɒ/
not	/ɒ/

b Look at the list of phonetic symbols on p127. Match the sounds and the words.

vowels		consonants	
/i:/	my	/h/	nice
/ɜ:/	please	/s/	this
/ɪ/	fax	/dʒ/	he's
/æ/	word	/m/	orange
/aɪ/	his	/ð/	man

c Compare your ideas with a partner. Practise saying the words.

2 Word stress

In words with more than one syllable, we usually stress only one of the syllables.

a 2.7 Listen and repeat.

stress on the first syllable	stress on the second syllable	stress on the third syllable
•Italy	A•merica	Argen•tina

b Write these words in the correct column.

telephone	Japan	hamburger	forty
umbrella	engineer	girlfriend	understand
lemonade	address	fourteen	architect

c Compare your ideas with a partner.

d 2.8 Listen, check, and repeat.

Extension Units 1 and 2

Language check

General review

1 Correct the sentences. Each sentence has one mistake.

EXAMPLE
How old you are? *How old are you?*
1 His in the garden.
2 Our car new is green.
3 I'm nurse.
4 That's Carl and her wife.
5 I'm twenty and one.
6 They no from Greece.
7 What means *umbrella*?
8 How you pronounce this?
9 That 70p, please.
10 Mr and Mrs Mills is on holiday.
11 A orange juice, please.
12 No look!

The verb *to be*

2 Complete the sentences with the correct form of the verb *to be*. Use short forms where possible.

1 A ~~He is~~ Mr Barnes here?
  B No, he *is not*. He *is* at a meeting.
2 A *Are* you from Poland?
  B Yes, I *'m*. I *'m* from Warsaw.
3 A Where *'s* the dog?
  B It *is* in the garden.
4 The two people over there *is* my parents. They *are* seventy-five years old.
5 A *Are* Jean and Marie married?
  B Yes, they *are*.

Plurals

3 Write the plurals.

singular	plural
watch	watches
woman	women
shop	shops
child	children
box	boxes
apple	apples
room	rooms
address	addresses

Numbers

4 Write the numbers.

81 *eightyone*   4 *four*
15 *fifteen*   12 *twelve*
40 *forty*   26 *twentisix*
33 *thertythree*   5 *fave*
97 *Nantyseven*   18 *eightyn*

Imperatives

5 Match the instructions and the pictures.

1 | c | Pick up your book.
2 | e | Look at this.
3 | f | Don't sit down.
4 | d | Come here, please.
5 | a | Open your book.
6 | b | Don't stand up.

Similar words

6 Choose the correct words.

EXAMPLE
We're / ~~Where~~ from France.
1 That's Sally's dog. *Its* / **It's** name's Muffin.
2 There's Maria and ~~here~~ / **her** new boyfriend.
3 A Where's Mark from?
  B *His* / **He's** from the USA.
4 A Where are Mr and Mrs Wilson?
  B *They're* / ~~There~~ over **there** / *their*.
5 He's *a* / *an* old man.
6 Is this *you're* / *your* book?
7 *I'm* / ~~Am~~ sixteen years old.

Conversations

7 **Complete the conversations with the expressions in the box.**

that's interesting	Yes, please
Anything else	he's fine
What do you do	Not bad
Small or large	And you
How do you do	be off
How are you	see you
Where are you from	

1 **Chen** Hello. I'm Chen.
  Selin *How do you*? I'm Selin.
  Chen Pleased to meet you, Selin.
  Where are you? from
  Selin I'm from Turkey. *And you*?
  Chen I'm from Singapore.
  What do you do?
  Selin I'm an architect.
  Chen Oh, *that's interesting*. My
    girlfriend's an architect, too.

2 **Pete** Hi, Lyn. *How are you*?
  Lyn I'm fine, thanks, Pete.
    And you?
  Pete *Not bad*, thanks.
    How's William?
  Lyn Oh, *he's fine*.
  Pete Well, I must *be off*.
  Lyn OK, *see you*.
  Pete Yes, bye.

3 **Assistant** *yes please*?
  Customer A hamburger and an
    apple juice, please.
  Assistant *Small or*? *large*?
  Customer Small, please.
  Assistant *Anything*? *else*
  Customer No, thank you.

Vocabulary

8 **Look at the Wordlist for Units 1
and 2.**
  Make questions and answers about
  ten words.
  EXAMPLES
  A How do you say Gracias in English?
  B Thank you.

  A What does teacher mean?
  B It means professeur.

Extra!
At a language school

1 📼 **A student is at a language school in London.
Listen and choose the correct answers.**

  1 What is the name of the language school?
    ☐ The George School of English
    ☐ The Edinburgh School
    ☐ The Gordon Language School

  2 Where is the interview?
    ☐ Room 6
    ☐ Room 16
    ☐ Room 60

  3 What is the student's name?
    ☐ Martina
    ☐ Maria
    ☐ Merinda

  4 What is the teacher's name?
    ☐ Peter Burton
    ☐ Piers Merson
    ☐ Paul Barton

2 **What can you remember?**

a Try to complete the card.

REGISTRATION

NAME ....

NATIONALITY ....

AGE ....

OCCUPATION ....

ADDRESS ....

....

TELEPHONE NO. ....

b Compare your ideas with a partner.
c 📼 Listen again. Check your ideas and complete the card.

3 **Work in groups of three.**
a Choose your roles: a new student, the receptionist, and the teacher.
b Make conversations for the student's first day.
c Change roles and make new conversations.

3 Descriptions

Grammar
have got / has got

Grammar in use

1 🔲 *3.1* **Read and listen to the conversation.**

Claire Have you got any brothers or sisters, Andrew?
Andrew I've got a sister, but I haven't got any brothers.
Claire Has your sister got dark hair, too?
Andrew No, she hasn't. She's got fair hair.
Claire What colour eyes has she got?
Andrew They're blue.

2 **Look at the pictures. Which person is Andrew?**

Rules

1 **Complete the table with short forms from the conversation.**

I You We They	have _'ve_		
	have not _haven't_	got	a sister.
He She It	has _'s_		
	has not _hasn't_		fair hair.

2 **Find questions with *have got* and *has got* in the conversation.**

a How do we make questions with *have got / has got*?

b Make these statements into questions.
You've got a brother.
_Have you got_____ a brother?
She's got brown eyes.
_~~Has she got~~_____ brown eyes?

3 **Look at the conversation again.**

a Complete these questions and answers.
A _Have_ you _got_ a sister?
B Yes, I _have_.
A _Has_ she _got_ fair hair?
B No, she _hasn't_

b How do we make short answers?

➤ Check the rules for *have got / has got* in **Grammar Reference 3.1**.

Practice

1 **Complete the description of Andrew and his sister.**
Andrew _has_ a sister, but he _has not_ any brothers.
He _has got_ dark hair, but his sister _has not got_ fair hair.
Andrew and his sister _have got_ blue eyes.

2 **Complete the sentences with *have got*, *has got*, *haven't got*, or *hasn't got*.**

1 Pilar _has got_ long hair.
2 Vera and Donatella _haven't_ long hair.
3 Pilar _hasn't got_ brown eyes.
4 Pilar and Vera _hasn't got_ dark hair.
5 Vera and Donatella _haven't got_ blue eyes.
6 Pilar _'s got_ blue eyes.
7 Vera and Donatella _____ brown eyes.
8 Donatella _____ long, fair hair.

Pilar

Vera

Donatella

3 **Work with a partner.**

a Ask questions and write down the answers.
Try to find out some details.

EXAMPLE
A *Have you got a pet?*
B *Yes, I have / No, I haven't.*
A *What have you got? What's its name? How old is it? What colour is it?*

	✓/✗	details
a pet	✓	*a dog, Spot, 8, black*
a computer		
a boyfriend / girlfriend		
a car		
a fax		
a mobile phone		
a garden		
a secretary		
a watch		
a camera		
a CD player		

b Find a new partner. Ask questions about his / her first partner.

EXAMPLE
A *Has Mario got a pet?*
B *Yes, he has. He's got a dog. Its name's Spot, it's eight years old, and it's black.*

Vocabulary
Describing people

1 **Look at the pictures.**

a Match the descriptions and the pictures.

brown eyes	a moustache	dark hair	glasses
long hair	a beard	fair hair	blue eyes
short hair	bald	green eyes	

b 🔊 **3.2** Listen and check your ideas.

c What do you notice about the word *bald*?

2 **Look at these ways of describing people.**

He's good-looking.
He's thin.
She's attractive.
She's slim.
They're ugly.
They're fat.
He's about 45 years old /
  He's middle-aged.

a Write these words in
the correct places.

quite	very	not very

_____ tall _____ tall _____ tall

b Think of someone famous (or find someone in this book) who
- is quite fat.
- is quite slim.
- is very good-looking.
- is not very attractive.
- has got very long hair.
- has got blond hair.
- is quite ugly.
- is very old.
- is about 50 years old.
- has got a moustache.

3 **Describe**
- a friend.
- a member of your family.
- a famous person.
- yourself.

EXAMPLE
My friend is about twenty-two years old. She isn't very tall.
She's very slim and she's quite attractive. She's got very dark
hair and brown eyes. Her hair is quite long.

Reading and writing
My family

1 **Read the text.**

My name's Ellen and my husband's
name is Peter. We've got three
children – two sons and a daughter.
Our sons' names are Ian and Ben.
They're twins, but they aren't
identical. Ian's got dark hair, but
Ben's hair is fair. Our daughter's
name is Tracy. She's eight years old.
The boys are four.

My father's name is Frank and my
mother's name is Maureen. I've got
two younger brothers, called Adam
and Bobby. Adam is married. His
wife's name is Ulrike. She's from
Sweden and she's got long, blond
hair. They've got a baby daughter
called Anna. So my parents have got
four grandchildren – two grandsons
and two granddaughters.

My husband's got an older sister,
but he hasn't got any brothers.
His sister's name is Millie. She's
still single.

a Write the names in the family tree.
b Are these sentences *True* (✓) or
False (✗)?

1 ☐ Frank is Ben's grandfather.
2 ☐ Peter's daughter has got
  black hair.
3 ☐ Adam is Bobby's brother.
4 ☐ Millie hasn't got a husband.
5 ☐ Bobby is married.
6 ☐ Peter hasn't got any sisters.
7 ☐ Frank and Maureen's
  granddaughters are twins.
8 ☐ Ben's brother has got dark hair.

c Check your ideas with a partner.

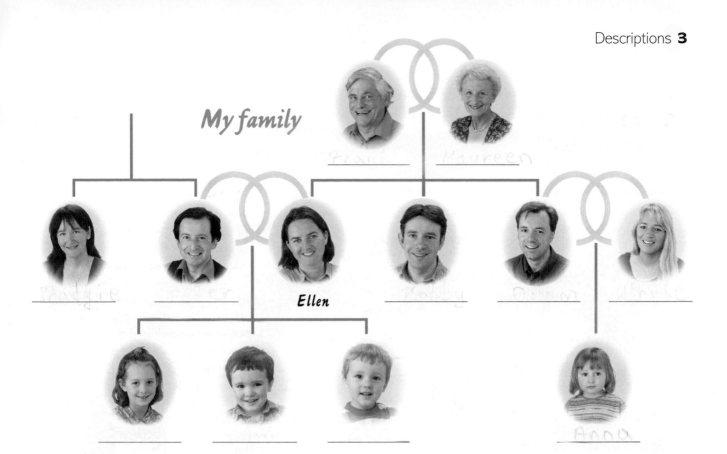

My family

Frank   Maureen

Millie   Peter   Ellen   Bobby   Adam   Millie

Anna

Vocabulary file: Families

a What do the underlined words mean?
Use the family tree to help you.
1 Adam is Ian's <u>uncle</u>.
2 Millie is his <u>aunt</u>.
3 Anna is his <u>cousin</u>.
4 Ian and Ben are Adam's <u>nephews</u>.
5 Tracy is his <u>niece</u>.

b Complete the table.

male	female
brother	sister
son	daughter
father	mother
uncle	aunt
nephew	
cousin	cousin
grandfather	granddaughter
	granddaughter

c 🔊 **3.3** Listen, check, and repeat.

Language focus: Possessive *'s*

a We call **'** an apostrophe. Look at this sentence.
What does *'s* show?
My husband's name is Peter.

b Look at these sentences. Which one is correct?
The boy's names are Ian and Ben.
The boys' names are Ian and Ben.

➤ Check the rules for the possessive *'s* in
Grammar Reference 3.2.

2 What is the relationship?
EXAMPLE
Ellen is Peter's wife.
1 Bobby is Anna _____ .
2 Tracy is Ben _____ .
3 Maureen is Ellen _____ .
4 Anna is Peter and Ellen _____ .
5 Ben is Millie _____ .
6 Anna and Tracy are Frank _____ .
7 Bobby is Ellen _____ .

**3 Ask your partner about his / her family.
Draw his / her family tree. Use these questions.**
- Have you got any brothers and sisters / children /
  aunts and uncles / cousins?
- What are their names?
- How old are they?
- Are they married?
- What are your parents' names?

4 Write a description of your family.

Listening and speaking
At the shops

1 Look at the picture. How many things can you name?

2 📼 *3.4* **Listen to the conversation and answer the questions.**
1 What does the man buy?
2 How much does each thing cost?
3 What colour is each thing?
4 What is his change?

3 📼 *3.4* **Listen again and check.**

Language focus: *this, that, these, those*

a Look at the pictures.

this watch	that watch
these pens	those pens

b Indicate and name some things in your classroom. Use *this, that, these,* and *those.*

EXAMPLES
This is my book.   *Those are the teacher's books.*

➤ Check the rules for *this, that, these, those* in **Grammar Reference 3.3**.

Conversation pieces: Shopping

a 🔊 *3.4* Listen to the conversation again.

b Match the two parts of the sentences.

Can	this black T-shirt?
How much are	have this T-shirt, please?
They're	be £18.75 altogether.
How much is	postcards?
It's	£10.50.
Can I	you are.
Anything	£7.25 each.
Have you got any	I help you?
I'll have	£1.25 change.
That will	those watches?
Here	else?
That's	these two, please.

c Look at tapescript 3.4. Read the conversation in pairs and check.

4 Work with a partner. Make conversations to buy two of these things.

➤ See **Functional Language: Shopping** p112.

Pronunciation
Vowel sounds (1);
-*es* endings

1 Vowel sounds (1)

Look at the list of phonetic symbols on p127.

a Match the words and the sounds.

one	/e/
two	/i:/
three	/ʌ/
four	/eɪ/
five	/ɔ:/
six	/ɪ/
seven	/u:/
eight	/aɪ/

b What are these words?

/seɪ/ _____
/tɔ:l/ _____
/faɪn/ _____
/blu:/ _____
/hi:/ _____
/mʌg/ _____
/sɪt/ _____
/red/ _____

c Compare your ideas with a partner.

d 🔊 *3.5* Listen, check, and repeat.

2 -*es* endings

a Tick (✓) the words that have an extra syllable in the plural.

✓	watch	watches
✓	badge	badges
☐	eye	eyes
✓	niece	nieces
✓	orange	oranges
☐	apple	apples
☐	telephone	telephones
✓	house	houses
✓	toothbrush	toothbrushes
✓	nurse	nurses
☐	uncle	uncles
✓	box	boxes

b Compare your ideas with a partner. Practise saying the words.

c 🔊 *3.6* Listen, check, and repeat.

d After which sounds is there an extra syllable?

4 Work and play

Grammar
can

Grammar in use

1  *4.1* **Read and listen to the interview.**

Interviewer Can you drive, Alan?
Alan No, I can't.
Interviewer Can you play a musical instrument?
Alan Yes, I can play the guitar and the piano. But I can't sing.
Interviewer Can you speak any foreign languages?
Alan No, I can't.
Interviewer Can you cook?
Alan Yes, I can.
Interviewer Can you play any sports?
Alan Oh, yes. I can play
football and tennis.
I can swim, too.
Interviewer Thank you.

2 **Complete the form for Alan.**

Summer Camp Leaders
• •

Name: Alan Wells . Sarah Ballaid

Tony Cooke

CAN YOU:

✓ ✗ **drive?** ✓

✓ soluton ✓ **play a musical instrument?** ✗
.......guitar /piano.......

✓ Grance sports ✗ **speak any foreign languages?** ✓
.....No I kon't.........french.

✗ ✓ **cook?** ✓

✓ ✓ **play any sports?** ✗
.....football / tennis......

✗ ✓ **swim?** ✓

Rules

1 **Complete the table with the negative form of *can*.**

I He She It We You They	can	swim.
	_____	cook.

2 **Look at the form. Say what Alan can and can't do.**
EXAMPLE
He can't drive.

3 **Look at the interview.**

a How do we make questions with *can*?

b Make these statements into questions.
Alan can swim.
_____ ?
You can play tennis.
_____ ?

c What are the short answers?
A Can Alan play the guitar?
B Yes, _____ _____ .
A Can he speak French?
B No, _____ _____ .

➤ Check the rules for *can* in **Grammar Reference 4.1**.

Practice

1 📼 *4.2* **Listen to two more interviews.**

a Complete the form for them.

b Check your ideas with a partner.

c Say what the people can or can't do.

2 **What can you do?**

a Use the **Vocabulary file**. Interview a partner.

b Form a group with another pair. Tell the group what your partner can or can't do.

EXAMPLE
Jan can play rugby and basketball, but he can't play golf.

3 **Complete the speech bubbles.**

> Help! I can't swim!
> I can't read that. I haven't got my glasses.
> Can I help you?
> Can you turn it up, please? I can't hear it.
> Excuse me. Can you speak English?
> Can I have these two postcards, please?
> Yes, I can. What can I do for you?

Vocabulary file: Free time

a Complete the words.

b Check your ideas in a dictionary.

c 📼 *4.3* Listen, check, and repeat.

sports I can play …

go_lf_   bask_et ball_   rug_by_

activities I can …

ri_de_ a bic_ycle_   sw_imin_   ski___

dri_ve_ (a car)   da_nce_   ru_n___

ri_de_ a ho_rs_   si_ng_   pa_int_

musical instruments I can play the …

vio_lin___   dr_oms_   saxo_phone_

d What is different about *play* with a sport and *play* with a musical instrument?

➤ Check your ideas in **Grammar Reference 4.2**.

e Write what you can and can't do.

EXAMPLE
I can play golf. I can't play basketball.

Vocabulary
Time

1 Look at the times.

a Complete them.

b 📼 *4.4* Listen, check, and repeat.

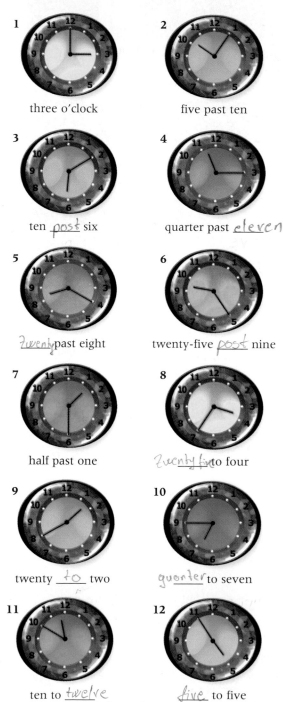

1 three o'clock

2 five past ten

3 ten _post_ six

4 quarter past _eleven_

5 _Twenty_ past eight

6 twenty-five _post_ nine

7 half past one

8 _Twenty five_ to four

9 twenty _to_ two

10 _quarter_ to seven

11 ten to _twelve_

12 _five_ to five

2 📼 *4.5* **Listen. What times do you hear?**

➤ See **Pronunciation: Reduced vowels** p31.

3 These are the days of the week.

Saturday	Thursday	Monday	Sunday
Tuesday	Friday	Wednesday	

a Write them in the diary.

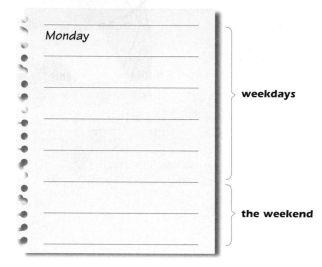

Monday

} **weekdays**

} **the weekend**

b 📼 *4.6* Listen, check, and repeat.

c Match the times and the parts of the day.

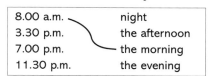

8.00 a.m.	night
3.30 p.m.	the afternoon
7.00 p.m.	the morning
11.30 p.m.	the evening

d What's your favourite day of the week? What's your favourite part of the day? Why?

4 📼 *4.7* **Listen to the conversations.**

a Complete the conversations with *in*, *on*, or *at*.

1 **A** Is the meeting _____ Friday?
   B Yes, that's right. It's _____ 3.30 in room 20.

2 **A** Is the conference _____ a weekday?
   B No, it isn't. It's _____ Saturday morning.
   A Oh, no. I can't go _____ the weekend.

3 **A** I've got an appointment at the doctor's _____ Wednesday.
   B Is it _____ the afternoon?
   A No, it's _____ the evening.

4 **A** Is your plane _____ 11.00 _____ the morning?
   B No, it's _____ 11.00 _____ night.

b 📼 *4.7* Listen, check, and repeat.

➤ See **Functional Language: Telling the time** p113.

Reading and writing
RU 18?

1 Look at the pictures. At what age can you do these things in your country?

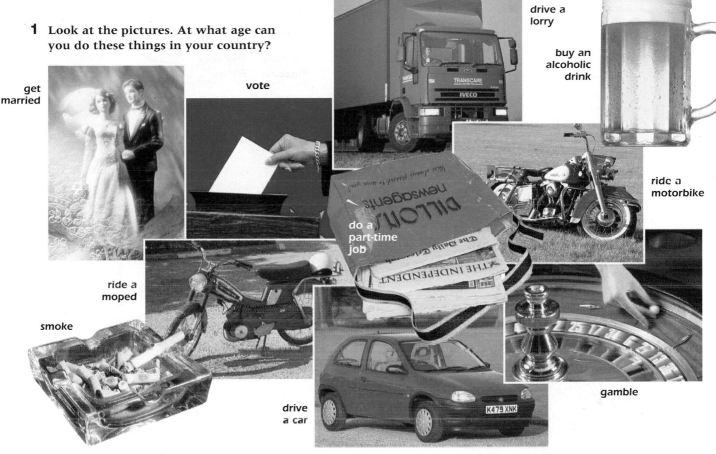

get married

vote

drive a lorry

buy an alcoholic drink

ride a motorbike

do a part-time job

ride a moped

smoke

drive a car

gamble

2 Read the text.

a At what age can you do things in Britain?

b Compare this to your own country.

▶ You can ride a moped when you're 16 years old, but you can't ride a motorbike or drive a car until you're 17. You can't drive a lorry or a bus until you're 21.

▶ You can't leave school and get a job until you're 16. You can do a part-time job when you're 13, but you can't work for more than 25 hours a week, and you can't work before 7 o'clock in the morning or after 7 o'clock in the evening.

▶ When you're 18 you can leave home and you can get married. (You can do these things when you're 16, if your parents agree.) You can also vote in elections when you're 18.

▶ You can go into a pub when you're 14, but you can't buy an alcoholic drink until you're 18. You can smoke at any age, but you can't buy cigarettes until you're 16. You can't gamble until you're 18.

3 Look at the things in exercise 1. What can these people do? What can't they do?
- Daniel is 17.
- Rebecca is 15.
- Jack is 19.

4 Do you think these are the right ages? Choose six things and write a sentence about each one.

EXAMPLES
17 is too young to ride a motorbike.
Why can't people vote when they're 16?

Language focus: *can / can't*

We use *can / can't* to talk about ability and permission.

EXAMPLES

ability *Jack can't buy a drink because he hasn't got any money.*

permission *Rebecca can't buy a drink because she's only 15.*

Listening and speaking
Jenny's week

1 ▦ *4.8* **Listen to the conversations.**
Which of these people does Jenny talk to?

- Sylvia
- the manager
- the dentist
- Stephen
- the dentist's receptionist
- Mark
- the manager's secretary

2 **What can you remember?**

a Complete Jenny's diary with these items.

> meet Mark   go to the dentist's
> play tennis   go to the BAC conference
> go to London

b Compare your ideas with a partner.

c ▦ *4.8* Listen again and check your ideas.

Language focus: *have to / has to*

a Look at tapescript 4.8. Complete these sentences.

I _____ to finish a report.

He _____ to go to Spain.

b Complete these sentences with *can't*, *have to*, or *has to*.

1 Jenny _____ play tennis on Saturday, because she _____ go to London.
2 They _____ play at 7.30, because Sylvia _____ make it at 6 o'clock.
3 Stephen _____ go to Spain, so he _____ go to the BAC conference.
4 Mark _____ make the meeting, because he _____ finish a report.
5 Mark and Jenny _____ meet on Wednesday afternoon, because Jenny _____ go to the dentist's.

c Write down five things you have to do this week.

EXAMPLE
I have to go to work.

➤ Check the rules for *have to / has to* in **Grammar Reference 4.3**.

Conversation pieces: Making arrangements

a Complete the expressions with these words.

good	make	it	right	about	Can
we	sorry	afraid	OK	on	

Suggesting

Can you play tennis at the weekend?

Can _we_ meet on Wednesday afternoon?

Is 10.30 _OK_ for you?

What _about_ Friday?

Can we make _it_ 7.30?

Accepting

Yes, that's OK.

Seven thirty's all _right_ for me.

See you _on_ Friday.

Yes, it's fine.

Rejecting

I'm _sorry_ I can't _make_ our meeting today.

No, I'm _afraid_.

Thursday's no _good_ for me.

b Check your ideas in tapescript 4.8.

c Work with a partner. Read the conversations.

3 Arrange a meeting

a Copy the diary.

b Make your own diary for next week. Write these things in your diary. Don't show it to anyone.
- doctor
- dentist
- go to (a meeting / New York / a conference)
- meet the manager
- finish a report
- go shopping
- have lunch with …
- write some letters
- read a report

c Work with a partner. Make arrangements to
- play a sport.
- meet for lunch.
- go to the cinema.
- spend a day somewhere.

➤ See **Functional Language: Arranging a meeting** p113.

Pronunciation
Vowel sounds (2); reduced vowels

1 Vowel sounds (2)

There are three types of vowel sound in English.

a Say these words.

short	long	diphthong
cat /kæt/	*can't* /kɑːnt/	*game* /geɪm/

b What type of vowels are in these words? Say the words and write them in the correct column.

got	/gɒt/	four	/fɔː/
fine	/faɪn/	pen	/pen/
fat	/fæt/	make	/meɪk/
boy	/bɔɪ/	three	/θriː/
car	/kɑː/	work	/wɜːk/

c Compare your ideas with a partner.

d 4.9 Listen, check, and repeat.

2 Reduced vowels

a 4.10 Listen and repeat these words.

can	/kæn/
to	/tuː/
at	/æt/
from	/frɒm/
are	/ɑː/

b 4.11 Now listen to these sentences. What happens to the vowels in the words above?
1 I can swim.
2 It's ten to six.
3 My appointment's at seven.
4 We're from Canada.
5 Are you Mr Jones?
6 Can you play tennis?
7 Are you from Spain?
8 We have to go at quarter to four.

c 4.11 Listen again and repeat.

d Practise saying the sentences.

e Write similar sentences of your own. Practise reading them to your partner.

EXAMPLES

I can sing.

It's five to five.

Extension Units 3 and 4

Language check

General review

1 Write the words in the correct order.

EXAMPLE

is she very not tall

She is not very tall.

1 dark has he hair got
2 brother quite my good-looking is
3 and you brothers got ? sisters have any
4 Bobby got hair has fair
5 much postcards these are how ?
6 you piano play ? can the
7 can't car I a drive
8 Wilson on to Berlin Mrs go has to Friday
9 to morning in it's four the twenty
10 is appointment ? half my eleven at past

Prepositions

2 Complete the time expressions with *in*, *on*, or *at*.

1 _____ 7.30
2 _____ night
3 _____ Monday
4 _____ the evening
5 _____ quarter to six
6 _____ Sunday afternoon
7 _____ the weekend
8 _____ 2 o'clock _____ Wednesday

Times

3 Write the times.

1 _____   2 _____   3 _____

4 _____   5 _____   6 _____

Short answers

4 Complete the short answers.

1 **A** Have you got a mobile?   **B** No, I _____ .
2 **A** Can you swim?   **B** Yes, _____ .
3 **A** Can Jenny drive?   **B** No, _____ .
4 **A** Has Peter got fair hair?   **B** No, _____ .
5 **A** Are you twins?   **B** Yes, _____ .
6 **A** Is this your car?   **B** No, _____ .

have or *has*?

5 Complete the sentences with *have* or *has*.

1 We _____ got a big house.
2 Tony _____ got a dog.
3 We _____ to go to work.
4 I _____ not got any sisters.
5 My friend _____ not got a car.
6 You _____ got beautiful eyes.
7 Suzie _____ to meet some visitors.

6 Rewrite the sentences using short forms if possible.

Conversations

7 Complete the conversation.

Darren _____ , Justin.
Justin Hi, Darren. _____ are you?
Darren I'm _____ , thanks. And _____ ?
Justin _____ bad.
Darren Listen. _____ you play squash _____ Tuesday evening?
Justin No, I'm _____ . I have _____ go to a conference on Tuesday. _____ about Wednesday?
Darren No, I'm _____ . Wednesday's _____ good for me. Can you _____ it on Thursday?
Justin Yes, Thursday's OK _____ me. _____ time?
Darren Is 7.30 _____ right?
Justin Yes, _____ fine. See _____ there at 7.30 on Thursday then.
Darren Yes, _____ you.

Vocabulary

8 Look at the Wordlist for Units 3 and 4.
Draw pictures of ten words.

Extra!
Making an appointment

1 Number the conversation in the correct order.

☐ **Mr Smith** It's Tom Smith.

☐ **Receptionist** Yes. Can you come at ten to three on Wednesday afternoon?

☐ **Receptionist** Thank you, Mr Smith. Goodbye.

☐ **Mr Smith** Yes, that's fine.

☐ **Mr Smith** Goodbye.

☐ **Mr Smith** Yes, can I make an appointment with Doctor Wall, please?

☐ **Mr Smith** No, I'm sorry. I can't. What about the evening?

1 **Receptionist** Good morning. Can I help you?

☐ **Receptionist** What name is it, please?

☐ **Receptionist** Doctor Wall isn't here in the evening on Wednesday, I'm afraid. I can put you in at half past six on Thursday evening.

2 🔊 **Listen and check.**

3 Work with a partner. Read the conversation.

4 Make new conversations.

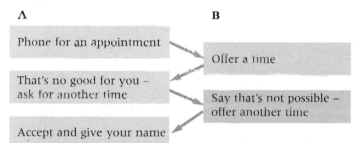

A

| Phone for an appointment |

| That's no good for you – ask for another time |

| Accept and give your name |

B

| Offer a time |

| Say that's not possible – offer another time |

Wild Thing

1 Read the song. Write these words in the correct places.

think	my heart
I love you	I want to know
love	everything
hold me tight	

2 🔊 **Listen and check your ideas.**

Wild Thing,
You make ___my heart___ sing.
You make ___everything___ move, baby.
Wild Thing.

Wild Thing, I ___think___ I ___love___ you,
But ___want to know___ for sure.
Ah come on and ___hold me tight___.
___I love you___.

5 Likes and dislikes

Grammar
The present simple tense

Grammar in use

1 📼 *5.1* **Read and listen to the conversations.**

2 **Match the conversations and the pictures.**

    1 **A** Do you like Shakespeare?
       B No, I don't.
       A Oh, that's a pity. I've got two tickets
           for *Hamlet*.

    2 **A** Do you want a drink?
       B Yes, please.
       A Tea or coffee?
       B Coffee, please. I don't like tea.

    3 **A** Do you like skiing?
       B Yes, I do. What about you?
       A It's all right, but I prefer snowboarding!

    4 **A** What about this restaurant?
       B Fine. I like Chinese food.

3 **Work with a partner.**
   Practise the conversations.

Rules

1 **The verbs in the conversations are in the present simple tense.**

EXAMPLES
I like Chinese food.
I prefer snowboarding.

a Complete this sentence from conversation 2.
I *don't like* tea.

b How do we make the negative form?

c How do we make questions? Write an example here.

_____ ?

2 **Find another example of**
- a positive statement
- a negative statement
- a question

3 **Complete the short answers.**

1 **A** Do you like this restaurant?
B Yes, _____ .

2 **A** Do you like rugby?
B No, _____ .

➤ Check the rules for the present simple tense in **Grammar Reference 5.1**.

Language focus: *like + -ing*

a Which sentence is correct?
I like ski.
I like skiing.

b Check your answer in conversation 3.

c Look at these verbs. How do we make *-ing* forms?

play	playing
drink	drinking
run	running
drive	driving

➤ Check the rules for *like + -ing* in **Grammar Reference 5.2**.

Practice

1 **Look at these things. Which ones do you like?**

swimming   cats   shopping

opera   golf   dogs

tennis   cooking   dancing

driving   learning English   pop music

a Write your ideas.

EXAMPLE
I like swimming. I don't like cats …

b Ask and answer with a partner

EXAMPLE
A Do you like swimming?
B Yes, I do / No, I don't. It's / They're all right, but I prefer …

2 **Look at these sentences.**

a Complete the sentences with *I* or *I don't* and the verbs in the box.

| speak | play | go | drive | like | prefer | drink | come |

1 *I drink* tea in the morning.
2 *I speak* three languages.
3 *I play* the piano.
4 *I prefer* radio to TV.
5 *I like* men with beards.
6 *I go* to school.
7 *I came* from Japan.
8 *I drive* a red car.

b Ask and answer with a partner.

EXAMPLE
A Do you drink tea in the morning?
B Yes, I do / No, I don't.

3 **Write sentences with your own ideas. Use *I (don't)* and the verbs in the box.**

| like | play | drink | speak | ride | buy | watch | prefer |
| smoke | come | read | write | work | cook | have to | |

Vocabulary
Food and drinks

1 Look at the spidergram.

a Write the names by the pictures. Use a dictionary to help you.

b 🔊 **5.2** Listen and check your ideas.

c Can you add any more words?

beer	mushrooms	wine	water	cheese
milk	eggs	rice	sausages	bananas
fish	sandwiches	bacon	grapes	bread
pasta	potatoes	tomatoes		

2 Work with a partner. Ask what he / she likes.

EXAMPLE

A *Do you like / eat / drink … ?*

B *Yes, I do / No, I don't.*

Reading and writing
What do you eat?

1 Ask your partner.

1 When do you have breakfast / lunch / dinner?

2 Which is your big meal of the day?

3 What do you have for breakfast / lunch / dinner?

4 What do you drink with your meals?

5 Do you go to restaurants or pubs?

2 Read the texts and complete the charts.

Betty and Phil

Meals	When?	What?
1 breakfast	7.30	toast cofee and orange-juice
2 *lunch*	1.30	salot, soup and asendwich.
3 *dinner*	9.30	

Roy and Joan

Meals	When?	What?
1 *breakfast*	5.30	bacon, sousagos, and eggs.
2 *lunch*	12.00	meat, pobato, vegateble.
3 *dinner*	5.00	

Language focus: Countable and uncountable nouns

a What is the difference between the two pairs of sentences?

This is an apple. I like apples.
This is cheese. I like cheese.

b Some nouns in English haven't got a plural form. We call these *uncountable nouns*. Look at the words in **a**. Which is uncountable?

c Read these conversations. When do we use *how much* and *how many*?

A I need some eggs.
B How many do you want?
A I need some rice.
B How much do you want?

d Work with a partner. Use the conversations in **c**. Ask and answer about the food and drinks on this page.

➤ Check the rules for countable and uncountable nouns in **Grammar Reference 5.3**.

You are what you eat

My name's Betty and this is my husband, Phil. We both work in offices in London. We have breakfast at half past seven. We don't have a big breakfast, because we have to go to work. We usually have toast, coffee, and orange juice.

For lunch we usually have a salad or soup and a sandwich. That's at about 1.30.

We have dinner at about half past seven. It's the big meal of the day and we have meat or fish with vegetables and potatoes, pasta, or rice. We have fruit or ice cream for dessert. We have a glass of wine with the meal. On Saturday evenings we usually go to a restaurant for dinner at about eight o'clock. We both like Chinese and Italian food.

I'm Roy and this is my wife, Joan. We live on a farm, so we have to get up early, at about 5.30. We start the day with a big breakfast – bacon, sausages, and eggs, with tomatoes and mushrooms. We have toast, too, and two or three cups of tea.

Our big meal of the day is lunch at 12 o'clock. We have meat with potatoes and vegetables, then a big pudding, such as apple pie and custard, and a cup of tea.

At five o'clock we have tea. That's a light meal – eggs perhaps, or cheese on toast, and then cakes or biscuits and another cup of tea! On Fridays and Saturdays we go to the pub in the evenings and have a few pints of beer.

3 **Read the texts again. Which couple is it?**
1 They drink coffee in the morning. _Betty and Phil_
2 They have breakfast at half past five. _R·J_
3 Lunch is their big meal of the day. _R·J_
4 They eat ice cream for dessert. _B·P_
5 They drink tea with their meals. _R·J_
6 They don't eat fish. _R·J_
7 Lunch is a light meal. _B·P_
8 They go to a pub at the weekend. _R·J_
9 They like Italian food. _B·P_

4 **Compare the information in the charts with your own meals. What differences are there?**

5 **Write about your meals.**

On weekdays I have breakfast at _10.00.o'clock_.
I usually have _a sandwiches_. *For lunch I have*
a pizza . *That's at* _2.00.o'clock_. *I have dinner*
at _6.00.o'clock_. *I usually have* _vegetables_ .
At the weekends _usually_ . *I like* _to go out_.

Language focus: *some* and *any*

a Look at the conversation.
 A *Have you got any cheese?*
 B *No, we haven't got any cheese, but we've got some ham.*

b Complete the rules with *some* and *any*.

We use __some__ in positive statements.
We use __any__ in negative statements and questions.

c Look at the spidergram on p36. What things have you got in your fridge at home?
 EXAMPLE
 We've got some beer. We haven't got any wine.

d Ask your partner about his / her fridge.
 EXAMPLE
 A *Have you got any beer?*
 B *Yes, we have / No, we haven't.*

➤ Check the rules for *some* and *any* in **Grammar Reference 5.4**.

Listening and speaking
'Would you like a drink?'

1 Look at the pictures. **Where are the people?**

2 **Read the parts of the conversations.**
a Write the conversations in the speech bubbles.
b 📼 5.3 Listen and check your ideas.
c Practise the conversations with a partner.

> That's £2.95, please.
> Mmm. That's a good idea.
> Here you are.
> Do you want ice and lemon in the mineral water?
> Thank you.
> Would you like a drink?
> I'll have a mineral water, please.
> A mineral water and a glass of red wine, please.
> Yes, please.
> What would you like?

3 📼 5.4 **Listen to some more conversations.**
1 What drinks do the people order?
2 Do they have anything in the drinks?

Conversation pieces: Offering and accepting

a Complete these expressions.

Would you _like_ a drink?

_Do_ you want ice and lemon?

What _do_ you like (to _drink_)?

I'll _have_ a cup of coffee, please.

_a_ cup of coffee, _please_.

b Look at tapescript 5.4. Practise the conversations in groups of three.

4 Work in groups of three. Make new conversations with this information.

- a glass of mineral water / ice and lemon / a glass of white wine / £3.10
- a cup of tea / milk / a cup of coffee / milk and sugar / £1.90
- a glass of red wine / a glass of orange juice / ice / £2.80

➤ See **Functional Language: Offering and accepting** p113.

Language focus: *Do you like / Would you like ...?*

a Look at the two questions. Which one is an offer?

Would you like a cup of tea?	No, thank you. Yes, I do.
Do you like tea?	Yes, please. No, I don't.

b Match the questions and the answers.

c 🔊 **5.5** Listen and give an appropriate answer.

EXAMPLES
A Do you like tennis?
B Yes, I do / No, I don't.
A Would you like a game of tennis?
B Yes, please / No, thank you.

Pronunciation
Consonant sounds; word stress: the /ə/ sound

1 Consonant sounds

a The phonetic symbols for most consonant sounds are the same as the letters.

EXAMPLES
dog /dɒg/
map /mæp/
sit /sɪt/

b Some sounds have special symbols. Match the sounds and the words. Use the list of phonetic symbols on p127 to help you.

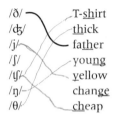

/ð/   T-shirt
/dʒ/   thick
/j/   father
/ʃ/   young
/tʃ/   yellow
/ŋ/   change
/θ/   cheap

c What are these words?

/kʌm/	_Come_	/fæks/	_fax_
/lɒŋ/	_Long_	/bædʒ/	_badge_
/ðə/	_The_	/wɒtʃ/	_watch_
/niːs/	_niece_	/juː/	_you_

d Compare your ideas with a partner.

e 🔊 **5.6** Listen, check, and repeat.

2 Word stress: the /ə/ sound

a Say these words. Mark the syllable with the stress.

EXAMPLES
doctor   Japan

doctor	dinner	about	breakfast	pizza
Japan	apple	lemon	address	afraid
bacon	salad	seven	water	pasta

b Compare your ideas with a partner.

c 🔊 **5.7** Listen, check, and repeat.

d 🔊 **5.7** Listen again. Underline the syllable with the /ə/ sound. Which syllable never has the /ə/ sound?

e The words are all nouns except *about*, *afraid*, and *seven*. Which syllable normally has the stress?

6 Daily life

Grammar
The present simple tense: third person singular

Grammar in use

1 Look quickly at the pictures and the text.
  1 Who is the man?
  2 What does he do?

2 Read the text again and match the two parts of the sentences.

Bob Wilkins works   to London by train.
He lives   from Belgium.
He communicates   the lifestyle in Belgium.
He travels   his job.
The train costs   in Belgium.
Bob enjoys   with the bank by e-mail.
He prefers   for a bank in London.
His wife comes   a lot of money.

Rules

1 Complete these sentences from the text.
Bob Wilkins **work** *for a bank in London.*
For two days each week I **am** *at home.*

a What do you notice about the verb in the first sentence?

b Find these sentences and complete them.
He **lives** *in Belgium.*
She **works** *in Brussels.*
It **costs** *a lot of money.*

c Complete this rule.

> In the third person singular (*he*, *she*, *it*)
> we add _____ to the verb.

d Complete these sentences with the verbs in the box.

> like   come   cost

  1 I **come** from England.
  2 My wife **comes** from Belgium.
  3 We **like** the lifestyle here.
  4 Bob **likes** his job.
  5 The train **cost** a lot of money.
  6 Houses **cost** less in Belgium.

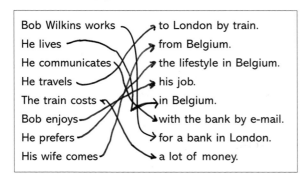

BOB WILKINS works for a bank in London, but he doesn't live in England. He lives in Belgium.

BOB: 'I don't go to the bank every day. For two days each week I work at home and I communicate with the bank by e-mail.'

On the other three days Bob travels to London by train, through the Channel Tunnel. It costs a lot of money, but he doesn't want to change his job because he enjoys it. So, why does he live in Belgium?

'Well, it's simple really,' says Bob. 'My wife comes from Belgium and she works in Brussels,

so one of us has to travel to work. We live in Belgium because we both prefer the lifestyle here.'

2 **Complete these sentences about Bob Wilkins with the verb *to live*.**

Bob _lives_ in Belgium.

He _doesn's_ in England.

a How do we make the negative form after *he*, *she*, and *it*?

b What happens to the *-s* on the verb?

c Find another example of a negative verb in the text.

3 **Find a question in the text.**

a What word do we use to make questions with *he*, *she*, and *it*?

b Complete the conversation.

A Where _does_ Bob work?

B He works for a bank in London.

A _does_ he enjoy his job?

B Yes, he _doesn't_

A _does_ he live in London?

B No, he _doesn't_

4 **Put in *-s* where necessary.**

1 Bob work_ in England.

2 His wife doesn't work_ in England.

3 Where does she work_ ?

➤ Check the rules for the present simple tense in **Grammar Reference 6.1**.

Practice

1 **Complete these sentences about Bob Wilkins. Use the verbs in brackets.**

1 Bob _works_ in England.
He _lives_ in Belgium. (live)

2 He _doesn't_ to work in Belgium.
He _want_ to work in England. (want)

3 He _doesn't_ in a shop.
He _work_ in a bank. (work)

4 He _doesn't_ to work every day.
He _go_ on Mondays, Wednesdays, and Thursdays. (go)

5 He _doesn't_ to work by car.
He _travel_ by train. (travel)

6 His wife _doesn't_ from England.
She _come_ from Belgium. (come)

2 **Read what Sandy says and complete the text.**

My name's Sandy.
I <u>live</u> in Milan, but I <u>don't come</u> from Italy. I <u>come from</u> the USA.
I <u>work for</u> a TV company. I <u>enjoy</u> my job and I really <u>like</u> the lifestyle in Milan, so I <u>don't want</u> to go back to the USA.

Sandy _lives_ in Milan, but she _dosn't come_ from Italy. She _comes_ from the USA. She _works_ for a TV company. She _enjoy_ her job and she really _likes_ the lifestyle in Milan, so she _doesn't want_ to go back to the USA.

3 **Look at the text about Sandy. Complete the questions and answers.**

A _Does_ Sandy _come_ from Italy?

B No, she _doesn't_

A Where _does_ she ~~is comes~~ from?

B She _comes_ from the USA.

A Where _Doesy_ she _works_ ?

B She _work_ for a TV company.

A _Does_ she _enjoy_ her job?

B Yes, she _enjoys Does._

A Where _does_ she _live_ ?

B She lives in Milan.

A _Does_ she _prefer_ the lifestyle there?

B Yes, _she_ _likes_ .does

A _Does_ she _want_ to go back to the USA?

B No, _she_ _doesn't_

4 **Find a partner.**

a Ask your partner about his / her lifestyle and write down the answers. Use this information.

EXAMPLE

A What do you do?

B I work in a shop.

- What / do?
- enjoy your job (or studies)?
- Where / live?
- play a musical instrument?
- like computer games?
- What / do at the weekend?
- cook the meals in your family?
- read a newspaper every day?

b Find a new partner. Ask questions about his / her first partner.

EXAMPLE

A What does David do?

B He works in a bank.

c Write about your first partner.

EXAMPLE

Maria works in a shop. She …

Vocabulary
Daily activities

1 **Read the text. Match the pictures and the verbs.**

Peter wakes up at seven o'clock, but he doesn't get up until 7.15. He has a shower and gets dressed. After breakfast he cleans his teeth. He leaves the house at eight o'clock and catches the 8.15 train to Manchester. On the train he reads the newspaper and does the crossword. He comes home at about half past six. After dinner, he washes up. Then he usually watches TV. He goes to bed at about 11.30.

wash up	do the crossword	clean your teeth	wake up
watch TV	have a shower	leave the house	go to bed
get up	catch a train	get dressed	come home

woke up
1

get up
2

a shower
3

get dressed
4

clean your teeth
5

6

catch a train
7

do the crossword
8

come home
9

10

11

go to bed
12

2 **Find these verbs in the text.**

a Write them in the spaces.

catch _____   do _____   go _____
wash _____   watch _____

b What happens to the verbs?

➤ See **Pronunciation: Present tense endings** p45.

3 **Describe your normal day.**

Reading and writing
It's a job, not a holiday

1 **Look at the pictures and read the first paragraph.**
  1 Who is the young woman? *isa chalet girl*
  2 Where does she work? *in Swidzeland*
  3 What does she do?

2 **Read the text. Are these sentences** *True (✓)* **or** *False (✗)***?**
  1 ☒ Monika goes to the shop at 5 a.m.
  2 ☒ She goes to the shop by car.
  3 ☑ The guests have coffee in bed.
  4 ☑ Monika tidies the chalet in the morning.
  5 ☒ She makes lunch for the guests at 12.00.
  6 ☑ The guests have cakes, tea, and wine at about five o'clock.
  7 ☒ Monika usually goes to a club in the evenings.
  8 ☒ She goes skiing every day.
  9 ☒ The new guests arrive on Saturday morning.
  10 ☑ Monika likes her job.

It's a job, not a holiday

Monika is a chalet girl. She works in the ski resort of Verbier in Switzerland. She looks after groups of skiers.

Her day always starts early. She gets up at 5 o'clock in the morning. At 5.30 she walks to the shop and buys some bread for the guests' breakfast. At 7 o'clock she makes some coffee and takes it to the guests in bed.

After breakfast the guests go skiing. Then Monika washes up, makes the beds, and tidies the chalet. She has a rest at about 11 o'clock. She doesn't make lunch for the guests, so in the afternoon she normally goes skiing for about three hours. At 4.30 the

3 **Here are the questions from an interview with Monika.**
- Where do you work?
- What time do you get up?
- What do you do first?
- What do you do after breakfast?
- Do the guests have lunch at the chalet?
- What do you do when the guests come back?
- What do you do in the evenings?
- Do you enjoy your job?
- Do you go skiing?

a Give Monika's answers.

b Think of three more questions and answers for the interview.

c Work with a partner. Roleplay the interview.

4 **Choose a member of your family or a friend. Write a magazine article about his / her job. Think about these things.**
- Who? What? Where?
- morning
- afternoon
- evening
- like the job? Why / Why not?

Language focus: Adverbs of frequency

a Put these words in the line.

| often | usually | always | sometimes |

never _____ _____ _____ / normally _____

b Find these sentences in the text.
Her day starts early.
She doesn't go out.
It's a very busy day.

c Put in the adverbs of frequency.

d Where do we put the adverb
- with a normal verb?
- with an auxiliary verb?
- with the verb *to be*?

e Put the adverbs in brackets into these sentences.
1 The guests are quite young. (usually)
2 They don't stay for more than a week. (usually)
3 Monika can't go skiing in the afternoons. (always)
4 Monika meets her friends on Sundays. (normally)
5 Monika makes lunch for the guests. (never)

f Write five sentences about your normal week. Use the words in **a**.

➤ Check the rules for adverbs of frequency in **Grammar Reference 6.2**.

guests come back and have some tea, cakes, and a glass of wine. Then Monika cooks the evening meal.

The guests often go to a café or a club after dinner. Monika sometimes goes with them or meets her friends, but she doesn't usually go out, because she has to get up early the next day. So she washes up and then she usually watches TV for an hour. She goes to bed at about 10.00.

Monika never goes skiing on Saturday, because it's always a very busy day. The guests leave in the morning and then Monika has to clean the chalet. After that she goes to the supermarket and buys food and other things for the week, before the new guests arrive.

Monika likes working as a chalet girl, because she meets a lot of different people. 'But,' she says, 'it's a job, not a holiday.'

Listening and speaking
Asking about times

1 Look at the pictures. What can you see?

2 When do these things normally happen in your country?

    1 When do shops open? When do they close?
Are they open every day?

    2 What is a normal working day?
What is a normal school day?

    3 When do banks usually open and close?

    4 What are normal office hours?

    5 What times do people usually eat?
When do restaurants and bars open and close?

    6 When are museums normally open?

    7 When do people normally get up?
When do they go to bed?

3 📼 *6.1* **Listen to the conversations.**

a Match the items in the columns.

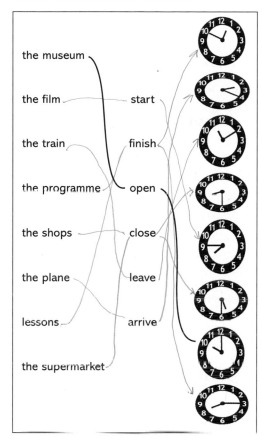

b Say what happens at each time.

EXAMPLE
The museum opens at ten o'clock.

4 **Work with a partner. Use the information in the chart and make conversations.**

EXAMPLE
A *What time does the museum open?*
B *It opens at ten o'clock.*
A *Thank you.*

5 **Work with a new partner. Make conversations with this information. (Make sure you use the correct singular or plural form.)**
- lessons / start / 8.15
- plane / leave / 4.25
- shops / close / on Saturdays / 6 p.m.
- film / finish / this evening / 11.10
- train / arrive / 3.50
- banks / open / on Mondays / 10.00
- the meeting / start / this morning / 12.00
- visitors / arrive / today / 3.00

Pronunciation
Voiced and voiceless sounds; present tense endings

1 **Voiced and voiceless consonant sounds**

These are voiced consonant sounds:
/b/ /d/ /g/ /v/ /ð/ /z/ /l/ /r/ /m/ /n/ /ŋ/

These are voiceless consonant sounds:
/p/ /t/ /k/ /f/ /θ/ /s/

a Do these verbs end in a voiced or a voiceless consonant sound? Write them in the correct column.

speak	live	sleep	sing	start	work	like
swim	dance	stand	meet	open	come	travel

voiced	voiceless
swim *live stand sing open come travel*	speak *dance sleep meet start work like.*

b 📼 *6.2* Listen, check, and repeat.

2 **Present tense endings**

We can pronounce the third person *-s* in two ways.

/z/	/s/
opens, gets, stands rides, comes arrives	looks, puts, gets, travels, looks, drinks speaks

a 📼 *6.3* Listen and write the verbs in the correct column.

opens	gets	puts	comes	likes	speaks
looks	stands	rides	travels	drinks	arrives

b Which sounds are followed by /s/? Voiced or voiceless?

c Say these verbs.

starts	wakes	lives	finds	meets	sings
reads	walks	drives	works	wants	thinks

d Some *-es* endings are pronounced /ɪz/. Tick (✓) the verbs which have the /ɪz/ sound.

☐ take	takes		☐ leave	leaves
☐ practise	practises		☐ finish	finishes
☐ wash	washes		☐ close	closes
☐ catch	catches		☐ do	does
☐ go	goes		☐ watch	watches

e 📼 *6.4* Listen, check, and repeat.

f Which spellings are pronounced /ɪz/?

➤ Check the rules for the pronunciation of present tense endings in **Grammar Reference 6.1**.

Extension Units 5 and 6

Language check

General review

1 Correct the sentences. Each sentence has one mistake.
1 I walks to school.
2 We no live in a city.
3 Ranjit don't work in a bank.
4 The shop close at six.
5 Ahmet washs the car on Saturdays.
6 When this programme finish?
7 They like ski.
8 I've got any money for you.
9 Do you like a glass of wine?
10 Does your husband prefers tea or coffee?
11 The bank doesn't closes until 4.30.
12 Do he come from Chile?

Present simple

2 Complete the conversations with *do*, *does*, *don't*, or *doesn't*.
1 A _Do_ you like basketball?
  B No, I _don't_.
2 A _Does_ your sister want to go to the party?
  B No, she _doesn't_
3 A _Do_ your friends go to Greece every year?
  B Yes, they _do_ .
4 A _Does_ Jason enjoy his job?
  B Yes, he _does_ .

Present simple questions

3 Write the questions.
A _Where do you work_? (Where / you)
B I work for a computer company.
A _Do you like your job_? (like your job)
B Yes, I do. I really enjoy it.
A _Where does your wife work_? (Where / your wife)
B She works at the university.
A _Does she teach_ ? (teach)
B No, she doesn't. She works in the library.

Present simple negative

4 Make these sentences negative.
1 My mother likes doing crosswords.
2 I go to bed early.
3 We travel to work by train.
4 Susan eats a lot of chocolate.

some or *any*?

5 Complete the sentences with *some* or *any*.
1 Have you got _any_ cousins?
2 We need _some_ bread for lunch.
3 I don't want _any_ sugar in my tea.
4 This water hasn't got _any_ ice in it.
5 I'd like _some_ water, please.

Adverbs of frequency

6 Put the adverbs in brackets into these sentences.
1 We get up at 9 o'clock on Sundays. (always)
2 He can finish work at four o'clock. (sometimes)
3 I don't get home before seven. (often)
4 She's late for meetings. (never)
5 They're on holiday in August. (usually)
6 Henri plays football on Saturdays. (normally)

Do you like / *Would you like* … ?

7 Tick (✓) the correct answer.
1 A Would you like a sandwich?
  B No, thank you. ✓
  B No, I don't.
2 A Do you like Switzerland?
  B Yes, please. ✗
  B Yes, I do. ✓
3 A Do you like cooking?
  B No, thank you. ✗
  B Not very much. ✗✓
4 A Would you like a cup of tea?
  B I'd prefer coffee, please. ✓
  B I prefer coffee.

Vocabulary

8 Look at the Wordlist for Units 5 and 6.

Make questions and answers about ten words.

EXAMPLES
A *What does **newspaper** mean?*
B *It means **giornale**.*

A *How do you say **manzana** in English?*
B ***Apple**.*

Extra!
Lifestyles

1 Look at the chart about
Saul Robbins' life.

2 🔲 Listen to an interview with
Saul. Choose the correct answers.

3 🔲 Listen again. What questions
does the interviewer ask?

4 Work with a partner.

a Look at the information in the chart.

b Ask and answer about Saul's life.
Student A asks questions 1–6.
Student B asks questions 7–12.

EXAMPLES
A Where does Saul live?
B He lives …

A What does he do?
B He's a …

5 Write about Saul's life.
EXAMPLE
Saul lives … He is a …
He works for … , etc.

6 Compare Saul's life to your own.
EXAMPLES
Saul lives … I live …
He is a … I'm …
He works for … , etc.

7 Work with a partner.
Use the other information
in the chart. Make another
interview.

1 live

2 do

3 work

4 go to work

5 do first

6 breakfast

7 travel to work

8 finish work

9 do after work

10 travel to other countries

11 like job

12 free time

7 Places

Grammar
there is / there are

Grammar in use

1 **A film director and his assistant are talking about a scene from a film.**
  1 Who are the people?
  2 What is happening?

2 **Read the conversation and choose the correct picture.**

Assistant In this scene the hero, Clint, comes out of the hotel and the bad guys attack him.

Director How many people are there in the street?

Assistant There are two men behind a car and there's a woman on the steps.

Director Is there anyone else in the scene?

Assistant No, there isn't. And there isn't any traffic in the street.

Director OK, great. So there aren't any problems with that. Now, what happens when the bad guys attack Clint?

Rules

1 We use *there is / there are* to describe a scene or place.

a Put these items into the table.

three people	a woman

There	is are	_____ _____	in the street.

b Find these things in the conversation.
  • the short form of *there is*
  • the negative forms

c Make these two sentences negative.
  There are two women in the street.
  There is a man on the steps.

2 How do we make questions with *there is* / *there are*?

a Find examples of questions in the conversation.

b Make these statements into questions and complete the short answers.

There are two men behind a car.

A _Are there_ ?

B Yes, there _Are_ .

There's a man on the steps.

A _Is there_ ?

B No, there _isn't_ .

➤ Check the rules for *there is* / *there are* in **Grammar Reference 7.1**.

Practice

1 Look at the picture. Complete the sentences with *There's, There are, There isn't,* or *There aren't*.

1 _There is_ a desk in the room.

2 _There are_ three pencils on the desk.

3 _Aren't_ two cats in the room.

4 _isn't_ a piano in the room.

5 _isn't_ a computer on the desk.

6 _is_ a newspaper on the floor.

7 _Aren't_ two pictures on the wall.

2 What can you remember?

a 🔲 *7.1* Close your book. Listen and answer the questions.

b Work with a partner. Compare your answers.

c Open your book. Look at tapescript 7.1 and check your answers.

3 Describe your classroom.
- How many people are there in the class?
- How many desks are there?
- Are there any pictures on the walls?
- How many windows are there?
- What is there on the teacher's desk?
- What else is there in the room?

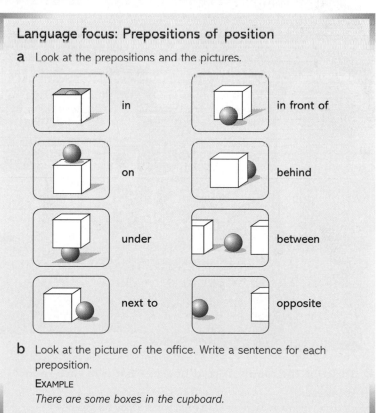

Language focus: Prepositions of position

a Look at the prepositions and the pictures.

in

in front of

on

behind

under

between

next to

opposite

b Look at the picture of the office. Write a sentence for each preposition.

EXAMPLE

There are some boxes in the cupboard.

Vocabulary
Parts of a house

1 **Look at the house.**

a What are the things in the rooms? Use the words in the chart.

living room	sofa television armchair coffee table bookcase
dining room	table chairs curtains
kitchen	fridge cooker cupboard sink washing machine
bedroom	wardrobe chest of drawers bed
bathroom	bath washbasin shower toilet mirror

b Can you add any more things to each room?

2 **Describe the rooms in your house. What is in each room?**

EXAMPLE
In the living room there are two armchairs. There's a sofa …

Reading and writing
Home sweet home

1 Look at the pictures. Do people live in places like this in your country?

2 Match the descriptions and the pictures.

3 Read the texts again.

a What reasons do the people give for liking / not liking their homes?

b What other advantages and disadvantages can you think of?

c Which place would you like to live in? Why?

4 Work with a partner. Ask questions about his / her home.
- in a city / town / village?
- flat or house?
- old?
- how many rooms?
- a garden?
- a garage?
- you / like?
- why / why not?

5 Write a description of your home (or your ideal home). Use the ideas above.

Home *sweet* Home

We live in Yorkshire, on a farm in the country. The farmhouse is quite an old building. It's about 250 years old, I think. There aren't many houses near us. There's a pub in the village about three miles away, but we're over twenty miles from the nearest town. That can be difficult for shopping, but we love it here. It's very quiet, there's no traffic, and the view is wonderful!

We don't live in a house or a flat. We live on a houseboat. The boat looks small, but it's quite big inside. Apart from the bathroom, it's only got one room, so we have to do everything there – eat, cook, sleep, and watch TV. We usually keep our houseboat at Little Venice in London. We're almost in the centre of the city there. That's great for clubs, pubs, the theatre, and so on. But the best thing about a houseboat is that you can move and take your home with you.

We live in a semi-detached house in a suburb of Manchester. We've got a living room, a dining room, and a kitchen downstairs. There's a loo downstairs, too. Upstairs there are three bedrooms and a bathroom. Outside there's a garage, a front garden, and a back garden. The house isn't very big but we like it. It's convenient for shops and schools and things like that, and the neighbours are very friendly.

I'm a student at Bristol University. I share a house with three other students. It's quite a big house. We've all got our own room. There's a bed, a desk, a chair, and a wardrobe in the room. It's got a washbasin and a mirror in the corner, too. We all share the kitchen, the living room, and the bathroom. We sometimes have arguments about things, like when someone spends too long in the bathroom, but we have a lot of fun, too.

Listening and speaking
'Excuse me. Where's ...?'

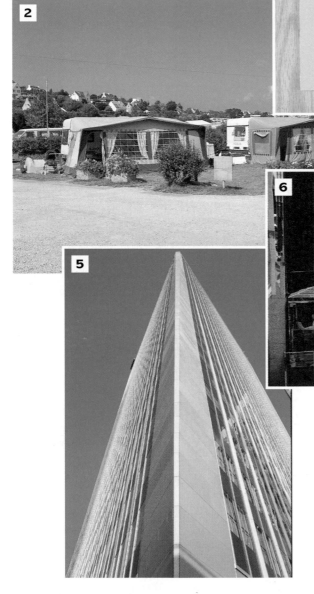

1 **Look at the pictures.**

a What do you think the conversations are about?

b 🔊 *7.2* Listen and check your ideas.

2 🔊 *7.2* **Listen again. Match the items and the pictures.**

first floor	third door
twenty-sixth floor	third level
seventh floor	second building

3 **Check your ideas with a partner.**

Language focus: Ordinal numbers

a Complete this list.

1st	_____	6th	_____
2nd	second	7th	_____
3rd	_____	8th	eighth
4th	fourth	9th	ninth
5th	_____	10th	tenth

b How do we make most ordinal numbers? Which ones are different?

c Look at this number.
23rd   twenty-third

d How do you think we say these numbers?
42nd   28th   31st

e Practise saying these numbers.
14th   29th   18th   11th   22nd   30th

➤ Check your ideas in the **Wordlist** on p117.

**Conversation pieces:
Asking where something is**

a Complete the expressions.

Asking where something is

_____ a post office here?

Where _____ find Mrs Wilson?

Excuse me. _____ the toilet?

Where can we _____ some bread for breakfast?

Saying where something is

It's _____ the first floor.

She's _____ Room 2654.

It's the third door _____ the left.

b Look at tapescript 7.2 and check your ideas.

c Read the conversations with a partner.

**4 Make new conversations with this
information.**

- reservation (name)?
  room 943 / 9th floor / lifts / opposite restaurant

- appointment / Mr Yamamoto / where?
  room 584
  5th floor?
  Yes / lifts behind you

- restaurant in the hotel?
  20th floor
  when / open for dinner?
  6.30

- where / Mrs Macdonald's office?
  upstairs / 2nd door / right
  lift?
  No / stairs over there

- where / get lunch?
  coffee house / 1st level
  how / get there?
  escalator / over there / coffee house / left

- where / gents / ladies?
  upstairs / door / left
  where / stairs?
  next to / bar

➤ See **Functional Language: Asking where
something is** p113.

Pronunciation
/ð/, /θ/; how many words?

1 The sounds /ð/ and /θ/

a 7.3 Listen. We can pronounce the letters *th* in two ways.

/ð/	/θ/
there *with*	*three* *seventh*

b Write these words in the correct column.

this	thick	third	their
mother	Thursday	father	ninth
think	the	through	they
both	then	these	thank you

c 7.4 Listen, check, and repeat.

d Say these sentences. How many /ð/ and /θ/ sounds are there in each sentence?

/ð/ /θ/

1 Is this the thirteenth floor? `2` `2`
2 The meeting's on Thursday at three thirty.
3 I think that's their mother.
4 The thick books are on the sixth shelf.
5 Thank you for those things.
6 There's Theo with his three thin sisters.

e 7.5 Listen and repeat.

2 How many words?

a 7.6 Listen to the sentences. How many words are there in each sentence? (Note: Short forms count as one word, e.g. *There's* = 1.)

EXAMPLE

1 It's twenty to three in the afternoon.

Number of words

1 `7` 6 ☐
2 ☐ 7 ☐
3 ☐ 8 ☐
4 ☐ 9 ☐
5 ☐ 10 ☐

b Compare your ideas with a partner.

c 7.6 Listen again and write the sentences.

d Work with a partner. Practise saying the sentences.

8 Entertainment

Grammar
The past simple tense: *was* / *were*

Grammar in use

1 Read the text.

a Answer these questions.
1 Where is it from?
2 Who is Stuart Stone?
3 What are the *Weekly Star* and the *Northern Mail*?

b Are these sentences *True* (✓) or *False* (✗)?
1 ☐ It was midnight.
2 ☐ Mitch's parents weren't in the house.
3 ☐ His sister was asleep in the next bedroom.
4 ☐ Mitch was eighteen years old.
5 ☐ He was often alone in the house.
6 ☐ There wasn't a telephone upstairs.
7 ☐ There was only one noise.
8 ☐ The noises were outside.

2 What do you think the noises were?

Rules

1 Look at the text.

a Complete these sentences.
Mitch _____ in bed. He _____ asleep.
His parents _____ at home.
They _____ away for the weekend.
There _____ a telephone downstairs.
There _____ definitely noises downstairs.

b Use the verbs in **a**. Complete the table.

I He She It	_____	out at work	yesterday.
We You They	_____	away at home	last week.

It was 12.30 on Friday night and Mitch was in bed. He was tired, but he wasn't asleep. His parents weren't at home. They were away for the weekend, and Mitch was alone in the house for the first time. It was very dark and quiet, but Mitch wasn't afraid. After all, he wasn't a kid any more. He was seventeen. What was there to be afraid of? And anyway there was a telephone downstairs, and ... What was that? And that? Were they noises? Or was it just his imagination? No, there were definitely noises downstairs. There was someone – or something – in the house with him!

'A great first novel. Don't read it alone!'
Weekly Star

'Definitely not for bedtime reading!'
Northern Mail

Noises in the Night

STUART STONE

imprint

2 Look at these sentences.

a Complete them.

She _____ on holiday last week.

They _____ at home yesterday.

b Make the sentences negative.

3 Find examples of questions in the text.

a How do we make questions with *was* and *were*?

b Put the words in the correct order to make a statement and a question.

Mitch / afraid / was

away / were / his parents

downstairs / a / there / noise / was

4 Change these conversations into the past simple tense.

A Is the film good?

B Yes, it is.

A Are there a lot of people at the party?

B No, there aren't.

➤ Check the rules for *was / were* in **Grammar Reference 8.1**.

Practice

1 Complete these conversations with *was*, *were*, *wasn't*, and *weren't*.

1 A _was_ you at Bella's party on Saturday?
   B Yes, we _were_ .
   A _Were_ Tim and Sara there?
   B Sara _was_ , but Tim _wasn't_ . He _was_ at a conference.
   A Oh? Where _was_ the conference?
   B It _was_ in Berlin, I think.

2 A _was_ there a phone call from Canada yesterday?
   B No, there _wasn't_ . There _were_ two from the States, but there _wasn't_ any from Canada. There _was_ a fax for you, too.
   A Oh, where _was_ it from?
   B It _was_ from Japan.

3 A _Were_ you out on Monday night?
   B Yes, I _was_ . Steve and I _were_ at the Wild Hearts concert.
   A _Was_ it good?
   B Yes, it _was_ .
   A _Were_ there any other bands on?
   B Yes, there _were_ , but they _weren't_ very good.

2 Look at the pictures.

a What places can you see?

b 🔊 *8.1* Listen. Where were the people yesterday?

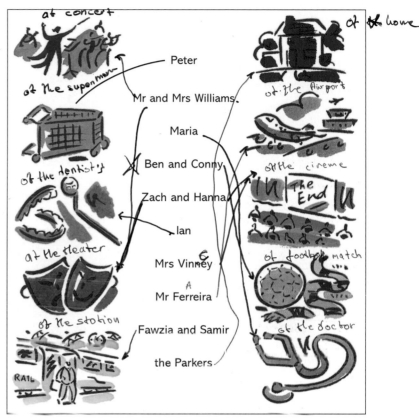

c Ask and answer about the people.

EXAMPLE

A Where was Peter?

B He was at the supermarket.

d Correct these statements.

EXAMPLE

Peter wasn't at the theatre. He was at the supermarket.

1 Peter was at the theatre.
2 Mr and Mrs Williams were at home.
3 Maria was at the cinema.
4 Ben and Conny were at a concert.
5 Zach and Hanna were at the supermarket.
6 Ian was at a football match.
7 Mrs Vinney was at the doctor's.
8 Mr Ferreira was at the dentist's.
9 Fawzia and Samir were at the airport.
10 The Parkers were at the dentist's.

3 Work with a partner. Ask and answer questions.

EXAMPLE

A Where were you last Saturday afternoon?

B I was at the shops.

- last Saturday afternoon
- at 7 o'clock this morning
- last Monday evening
- at 11.30 last night
- on Sunday morning
- two hours ago
- at 4.00 p.m. yesterday
- on your last birthday

Vocabulary
Giving dates

1 These are the months of the year.

☐ March	☐ November
☐ January	☐ June
☐ May	☐ December
☐ August	☐ September
☐ October	☐ February
☐ July	☐ April

a Can you number them in the correct order?

b Compare your ideas with a partner.

c 📼 *8.2* Listen, check, and repeat.

2 Look at this rule.

> We write *23 November*
>   or *November 23.*
> We say *the twenty-third of November*
>   or *November the twenty-third.*

a 📼 *8.3* Listen. What dates do you hear?

b 📼 *8.3* Listen again and write the dates.

c Work with a partner. Practise saying the dates.

d Which of these prepositions do we use with dates?

in	on	at

3 Go round the class. Find the person whose birthday is closest to your own.

EXAMPLE
A *When's your birthday?*
B *It's on the thirteenth of June.*

4 Write down five other dates that are important to you. Tell your partner about them.

EXAMPLE
7 January is my parents' wedding anniversary.

➤ See **Functional Language: Dates** p114.

Reading and writing
It was a busy week

1 Look at the noticeboard. What are the couple's names?

2 Look at the noticeboard **quickly** and answer these questions.

1 What's the dentist's name?
2 Who was the dental appointment for?
3 Who was at the conference?
4 When was the football match?
5 What does the woman do on Saturdays?
6 What was the name of the play?
7 Where was the party?

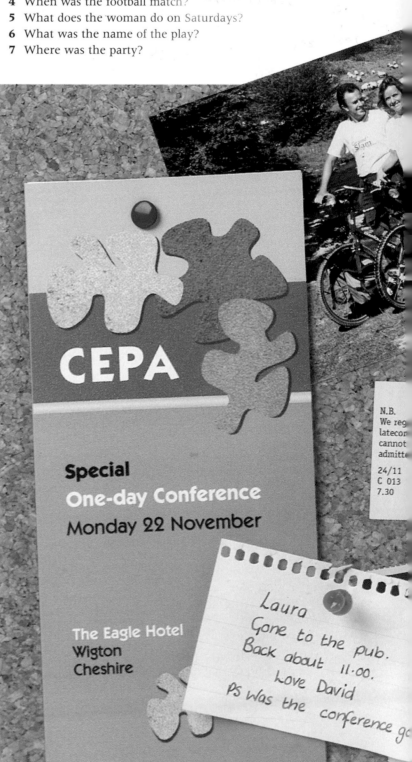

N.B.
We reg
latecor
cannot
admitt

24/11
C 013
7.30

Special
One-day Conference
Monday 22 November

The Eagle Hotel
Wigton
Cheshire

Laura
Gone to the pub.
Back about 11·00.
Love David
PS Was the conference go

3 Last week was a busy week. Read the items on the noticeboard.

a Complete the calendar. Which day was free?

b Describe the week.

EXAMPLE

On Monday Laura was …

4 Complete these sentences with *was, wasn't, were,* or *weren't.*
1 The conference _____ at the Eagle Hotel.
2 David's dental appointment _____ in the morning.
3 David and Laura _____ at the theatre on Thursday.
4 They _____ at Pete and Rosy's place on Friday evening.
5 They _____ both at the football match.
6 Laura _____ at home on Saturday evening.
7 The tickets for the theatre _____ £12.70 each.
8 On Tuesday afternoon David _____ in Manchester.

5 Imagine that last week was very busy for you.

a Write a description of your week.

EXAMPLE

On Monday I was at work all day. In the evening my girlfriend / boyfriend and I were at the cinema. On Tuesday morning …

b Work with a partner. Ask and answer questions about his / her week.

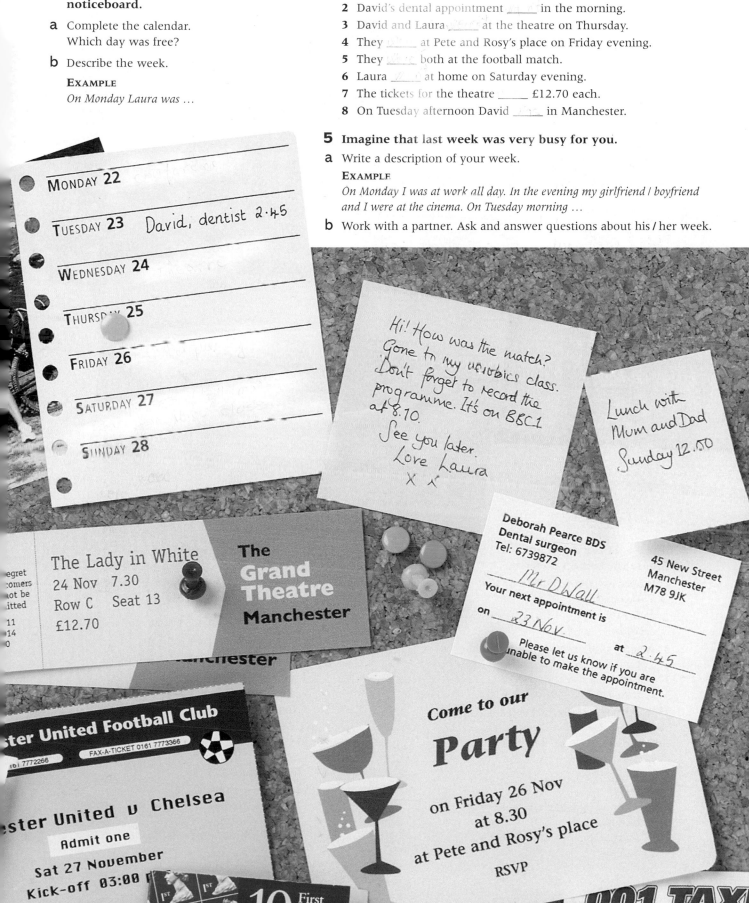

MONDAY 22

TUESDAY 23   David, dentist 2.45

WEDNESDAY 24

THURSDAY 25

FRIDAY 26

SATURDAY 27

SUNDAY 28

Hi! How was the match? Gone to my aerobics class. Don't forget to record the programme. It's on BBC1 at 8.10. See you later. Love Laura x x

Lunch with Mum and Dad Sunday 12.00

The Lady in White
The **Grand Theatre** Manchester
24 Nov   7.30
Row C   Seat 13
£12.70

Deborah Pearce BDS
Dental surgeon
Tel: 6739872
Mr D Wall
Your next appointment is
on   *23 Nov*   at   *2.45*
Please let us know if you are unable to make the appointment.

45 New Street
Manchester
M78 9JK

ster United Football Club
FAX-A-TICKET 0161 7773366
ster United v Chelsea
Admit one
Sat 27 November
Kick-off 03:00

Come to our
Party
on Friday 26 Nov at 8.30 at Pete and Rosy's place
RSVP

10 First Class Stamps

001 TAXI
(CITY CENTRE WAITING ROOM
* Zero meter on pick-up
* No surcharge outside city
* Account customers welcome
* Discount on long journeys

Listening and speaking
WOMAD

1 Look at the pictures.

a What do you think *WOMAD* stands for?
World of M_____ , A_____ , and D_____ .

b 🔊 *8.4* Listen to the conversation and check your ideas.

2 🔊 *8.4* **Listen again and choose the correct answers.**

1 Where was the festival?
   ✓ ☐ Reading
   ☐ Bristol
   ☐ York

2 Where was Karen's favourite band from?
   ✓ ☐ Uganda
   ☐ Colombia
   ☐ Korea

3 Which kind of food doesn't she mention?
   ✓ ☐ North African
   ✓ ☐ Mexican
   ☐ Turkish
   ✓ ☐ Japanese
   ✓ ☐ Indian

4 How many people were there?
   ☐ hundreds
   ✓ ☐ thousands
   ☐ a million

5 What was the weather like at the festival on Saturday morning?
   ✗ ☐ dry and sunny
   ✗ ☐ cold and wet
   ✓ ☐ cloudy but warm

6 What was the weather like on Sunday?
   ☐ dry and sunny
   ✓ ☐ cold and wet
   ☐ cloudy but warm

7 Where were they?
   ✗ ☐ in a tent
   ☐ in a hotel
   ✓ ☐ in a caravan

8 How long were they there?
   ✓ ☐ Friday to Sunday
   ✓ ☐ only on Saturday
   ✗ ☐ Saturday and Sunday

3 Describe Karen and Josh's weekend.

EXAMPLE
Karen and Josh were at a music festival in …

Conversation pieces: Responding

a Match the two parts of these expressions from the conversation.

Oh,	great.
Oh, I	it wasn't.
It sounds	see.
Oh, that's	really?
No, I bet	a pity.

b Check your ideas in tapescript 8.4.

---

4 **Talk about your weekend with a partner.**

a 📟 *8.4* Listen to the conversation again. What questions does Ben ask?

b Choose one of the events below. One of you was at the event. Use the questions in **a** and make the conversation.
- a wedding
- a sports event
- a party
- a rock concert
- a motor show

Vocabulary file: Weather

a Use a dictionary. Match the words and the symbols.

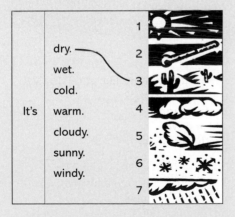

It's
dry.
wet.
cold.
warm.
cloudy.
sunny.
windy.

b Describe the weather in your country.
- today
- yesterday
- last week
- in May
- in December

Pronunciation
/ɪ/, /iː/; **words ending in -*e***

1 **The sounds /ɪ/ and /iː/**

a 📟 *8.5* Listen. Is it the same sound or different? Tick the boxes.

	1	2	3	4	5	6	7	8
same	☐	☐	☐	☐	☐	☐	☐	☐
different	☐	☐	☐	☐	☐	☐	☐	☐

b 📟 *8.6* Listen. Number the words in the order that you hear them.

☐ thin	☐ key	☐ tea
☐ slim	☐ green	☐ pink
☐ swim	☐ ski	☐ three

c 📟 *8.6* Listen again and repeat.

d Say these sentences. How many /ɪ/ and /iː/ sounds are there in each sentence?

		/ɪ/	/iː/
1	These are his skis.	1	2
2	She's his twin.	☐	☐
3	Listen to these three things.	☐	☐
4	Is he sixteen?	☐	☐
5	We have to meet the visitors.	☐	☐
6	He's in room six.	☐	☐

e 📟 *8.7* Listen and repeat.

2 **Words ending in -*e***

a Look at these words. How many syllables has each word got? Write the words in the correct column.

couple	bicycle	home	date
were	sentence	village	double
centre	where	time	exercise
opposite	theatre	score	change
make	people	eagle	conference

1	2	3
were	*couple*	

b 📟 *8.8* Listen, check, and repeat.

c Look at the words. When is the -*e* ending pronounced as a separate syllable?

Extension Units 7 and 8

Language check

Dates

1 Write the dates as we say them.

EXAMPLE

27/7   *the twenty-seventh of July*

30/1 _____

 1/9 _____

23/2 _____

18/8 _____

5/11 _____

12/6 _____

 2/4 _____

26/5 _____

Is there? / Are there?

2 Complete the questions.

1 _____ thirty students in our class?

2 _____ a meeting today?

3 How many people _____ here?

4 _____ a telephone near here?

5 _____ any apples in the cupboard?

Prepositions

3 Look at the picture. Complete the sentences with *There's* or *There are* and the correct preposition.

1 _____ a computer _____ the desk.

2 _____ three books _____ the computer.

3 _____ box _____ the desk.

4 _____ seven disks _____ the box.

5 _____ a dog _____ the desk and the chair.

6 _____ six CDs _____ the stereo.

7 _____ a picture _____ the wall.

8 _____ a glass _____ the computer.

was / were

4 Complete the conversation.

Sue Were you at the party last Saturday?

Alex Yes, I was.

Sue Was it at Judy's place?

Alex No, it wasn't It was at Sara's.

Sue Were there a lot of people there?

Alex No, weren't. There were only about twenty.

Sue Was Peter there?

Alex Yes, He was .

Sue Was he with his girlfriend?

Alex No, he wasn't She wasn't there.

Sue Was there a lot of food?

Alex Yes, there was And it was wonderful!

Conversations

5 Correct the mistakes. There is a mistake in each line.

1 **A** Excuse.
  B Yes? I can help you?
  A Where I find Mr Long?
  B He's at the sixth floor.
  A Thank you. Where's lift?
  B He's over there.

2 **A** Is a telephone near here?
  B Yes, there is. Is downstairs.

3 **A** Were you away the weekend?
  B Yes, we was.
  A Where you were?
  B We were at Paris.
  A Oh, real?
  B Yes, it was our anniversary of wedding.
  A What like was the weather?
  B It was warm but cloud.

4 **A** Do you like your place new?
  B Yes, we do. It's a quite big house.
  A How much rooms has it got?
  B It's got a living room, a kitchen, a bathroom, and two bed rooms.
  A Has got a garden?
  B Yes, it has got.

Vocabulary

6 Look at the Wordlist for Units 7 and 8.

Write definitions for ten words.

EXAMPLES

July   *It's the seventh month.*

kitchen   *It's the room where you cook food.*

Extra!
Witness

1 **Look at the picture. There was a robbery at the shop and a customer is trying to remember the scene, but there are some mistakes.**

a Listen and find the mistakes.

b Compare your ideas with a partner.

c Listen again and check your ideas.

2 **Write down the mistakes.**

EXAMPLE

It wasn't half past ten. It was ten o'clock.

You've got to hide your love away

1 Read the words of the song. How does the singer feel?

2 Listen to the song.

3 Look at the examples in the song. Connect the words that rhyme.

4 Listen again and check your ideas.

5 Look at the pairs of rhyming words.

a Do the words have the same spelling?

b Can you think of another word that rhymes with each pair?

Here I stand, head in hand,
Turn my face to the wall.
If she's gone I can't go on,
Feeling two foot small.
Everywhere people stare,
Each and every day.
I can see them laugh at me,
And I hear them say,

Hey, you've got to hide your love away.
Hey, you've got to hide your love away.

How can I even try?
I can never win.
Hearing them and seeing them,
In the state I'm in.
How can she say to me,
'Love will find a way'?
Gather round all you clowns,
Let me hear you say . . .

9 Survivors

Grammar
The past simple tense: regular verbs

Grammar in use

1 Look at the picture and the conversation. Who are the three people?

2 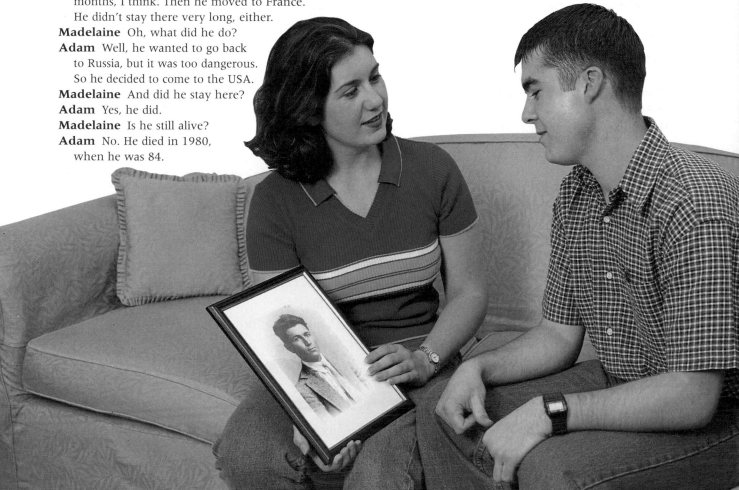 *9.1* Read and listen to the conversation. Choose the countries that Alexei lived in, and put them in the correct order.

☐ the USA
☐ Spain
☐ Canada
☐ Sweden
☐ Russia
☐ Argentina
☐ France

Madelaine Who's this?
Adam That's my great-grandfather, Alexei. He was born in Russia, but after the Revolution he moved to Sweden.
Madelaine Did he stay in Sweden?
Adam No, he didn't. He stayed there for only a few months, I think. Then he moved to France. He didn't stay there very long, either.
Madelaine Oh, what did he do?
Adam Well, he wanted to go back to Russia, but it was too dangerous. So he decided to come to the USA.
Madelaine And did he stay here?
Adam Yes, he did.
Madelaine Is he still alive?
Adam No. He died in 1980, when he was 84.

Rules

1 The conversation uses the past simple tense.

a Find the past simple forms of these verbs. Write them in the table.

present	past
stay	_____
want	_____
move	_____
decide	_____
die	_____

b How do we make the past simple tense?

c 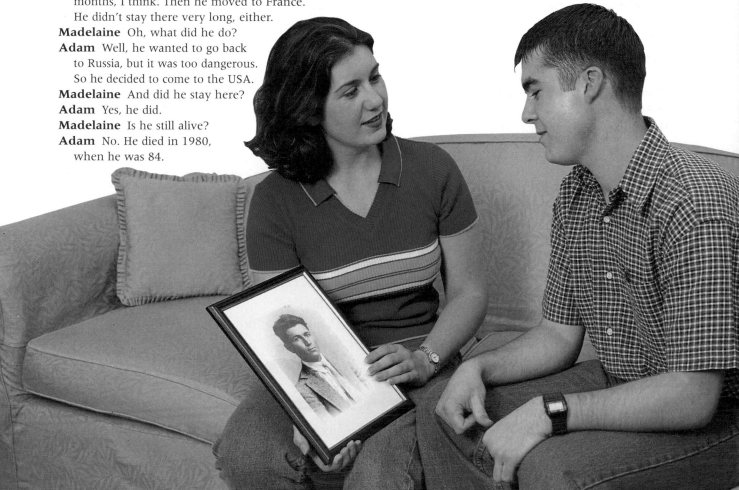 *9.1* Listen to the conversation again. What do you notice about the verbs *want* and *decide*?

➤ See **Pronunciation: *-ed* endings** p67.

2 Complete these sentences from the conversation.

He _____ there for only a few months.

_____ he _____ in Sweden?

He _____ there very long.

a How do we make questions and negatives in the past simple tense?

b Which part of the verb do we use after *did* or *didn't*?

3 Choose the correct form of the verbs.

1 'Did he | liked / like | Sweden?' 'Yes, he | did. / liked.'

2 'Did he | stay / stayed | in France?' 'No, he | didn't. / didn't stay.'

3 He didn't | wanted / want | to leave Russia.

➤ Check the rules for the past simple tense: regular verbs in **Grammar Reference 9.1**.

Practice

1 Adam is talking about his great-grandfather. Put the verbs in brackets into the past simple tense.

1 He _____ (want) to stay in Russia, but it _____ (be) too dangerous.

2 When he _____ (be) in France, he _____ (work) in a factory.

3 When he _____ (arrive) in the USA, he _____ (live) in Boston.

4 But then he _____ (move) to Los Angeles in California.

5 He _____ (like) California, so he _____ (decide) to stay there.

6 Later he _____ (open) a music shop.

7 When he _____ (be) an old man, he _____ (return) to Russia for a holiday.

8 He _____ (die) before I _____ (be) born.

2 Make these sentences negative.

1 Alexei wanted to leave Russia.

2 He stayed in Sweden for a long time.

3 He lived in England for two years.

4 He worked in a hotel in Paris.

5 He enjoyed his job in France.

6 He travelled to the USA by plane.

7 He liked Boston.

8 He moved to San Francisco.

9 He started a film company.

10 He died when Adam was two years old.

3 Adam and Madelaine are talking about Adam's great-grandmother.

a Make Madelaine's questions.

die before you were born?	stay there?
Where / live in the USA?	born in the USA?
want to work in films?	succeed?
Why / decide to leave Ireland?	
When / her family move to the States?	

Adam This is my great-grandmother, Sheena.
Madelaine _____
Adam No, she wasn't. She was born in Ireland.
Madelaine _____
Adam Her parents moved there when Sheena was still a child.
Madelaine _____
Adam They wanted to find a better life.
Madelaine _____
Adam They lived in New York when they first arrived.
Madelaine _____
Adam Her parents did, but Sheena decided to go to Hollywood.
Madelaine _____
Adam Yes, she wanted to be an actress.
Madelaine _____
Adam No, she didn't. Then she married my great-grandfather, Alexei.
Madelaine _____
Adam No, she didn't. She died when she was 96, so I can remember her.

b 9.2 Listen and check your answers.

4 Write about Adam's great-grandmother.

EXAMPLE

Adam's great-grandmother's name was Sheena. She was born …

5 Write a story about one of your ancestors (real or imaginary).

Vocabulary
Verbs

1 Match the verbs and the pictures.
Use a dictionary to help you.

slip
grab
cry
fall
climb
hold
lift
hurry
jump
talk
whisper
wave

2 Complete these sentences. Use verbs from exercise 1 in the past tense.
1 I _____ out of the house and _____ on the bus.
2 The little boy _____ when someone _____ his ice cream.
3 'I love you,' she _____ , and then she _____ goodbye.
4 I _____ the bag, but it was very heavy and it _____ out of my hands.

3 Some verbs in English have two parts.
Match the verbs and the pictures.

| look back | look up | look down |

Reading and writing
Chairlift terror

1 Look at the picture and find these things.
Use a dictionary to help you.

| chair | chairlift operator | helicopter | coat | the ground |

2 Look quickly at the paragraphs.
1 Who are the woman and the boy?
2 Where did the accident happen?
3 Did the boy fall?

3 Read the paragraphs.
Number them in the correct order.

Chairlift *terror*

☐ Then suddenly the chairlift stopped and Luke slipped from the chair. Fran grabbed his hand and stopped him just in time. She tried to pull the child back into the chair, but he was too heavy. 'Help! Help!' she shouted.

☐ But Luke didn't fall. The chairlift operator climbed up to the chair and helped Fran to hold her son. About five minutes later the police helicopter arrived and lifted Luke into the chair.

☐ People looked up and screamed. Luke was 20 metres above the ground. Someone telephoned for a helicopter and people hurried to put coats on the ground under the boy.

☐ It was a normal day at the Dreamland theme park in Wellington, New Zealand, and young Luke Mansen wanted to go on the Skyrider chairlift. With his mother, Fran, he waited for a chair. When it arrived, he jumped in and Fran followed him.

☐ Everybody watched and waited while up in the chair Fran talked to Luke: 'Don't look down, Luke. Hold on.' Every second was like a lifetime and the child started to cry. 'I can't hold on,' he whispered. 'Goodbye, Mum.'

☐ The chair moved out into the sunshine. It was a warm, sunny day, so there were thousands of people at the park. As the chair lifted Fran and Luke up into the sky they looked down, and Luke waved to the people on the ground. It was Luke's first time in a chairlift and he was very excited.

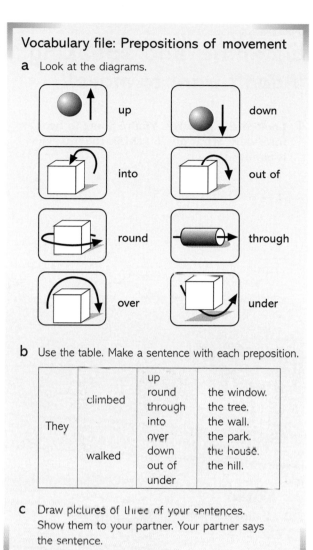

Vocabulary file: Prepositions of movement

a Look at the diagrams.

● ↑	up	● ↓	down
into	into	out of	out of
round	round	through	through
over	over	under	under

b Use the table. Make a sentence with each preposition.

They	climbed	up	the window.
		round	the tree.
		through	the wall.
		into	the park.
	walked	over	the house.
		down	the hill.
		out of	
		under	

c Draw pictures of three of your sentences. Show them to your partner. Your partner says the sentence.

4 A TV reporter interviewed Fran.

a Here are the questions. Write Fran's answers.
1 Why did Luke slip from the chair?
2 How did you stop him?
3 Why didn't you pull him back into the chair?
4 How high up were you?
5 What did the people on the ground do?
6 Did Luke cry?
7 How did the chairlift operator help you?
8 What did the helicopter do?

b Work with a partner. Roleplay the interview.

Language focus: Past simple tense spelling

a Find the past tenses of these verbs in the story.

slip _____   try _____
grab _____   hurry _____

b What do you notice about the spelling?

➤ Check your ideas in **Grammar Reference 9.1**.

Listening and speaking
'I don't want to move!'

1 Look at the pictures. You're going to hear an interview. What do you think the interview is about?

2 📼 *9.3* **Listen to the introduction.**

a Choose the correct answers.

1 What is the woman's name?
☐ Eileen
☐ Ida
☐ Morna

2 What is the name of her house?
☐ Orchard Cottage
☐ Riverside Cottage
☐ Bramble Cottage

3 What is Sainsbury's?
☐ a supermarket
☐ a hotel
☐ a property company

4 What did they want to do?
☐ to sell her cottage
☐ to move her cottage
☐ to knock down her cottage

5 When did it happen?
☐ last year
☐ two months ago
☐ two years ago

6 How old is the woman?
☐ 69
☐ 75
☐ 79

b How did the woman feel about the plan?

Language focus: *ago*

Look at this sentence.
They wanted to buy the land two years ago.

a Compare it with your language.

b Answer these questions with *ago*.
1 When were you born?
2 When was your last holiday?
3 When did you start learning English?
4 When did the dinosaurs die out?
5 When did you have breakfast?
6 When did this lesson start?
7 When did you start this book?
8 When did you last play any sport?

➤ Check the rules for *ago* in **Grammar Reference 9.2**.

3 9.3 **Listen to the interview.**

a What happened?

b 9.3 Listen again and complete these sentences.
1 Why did Sainsbury's ____ ____ ____ ____ ____ ?
2 How much ____ ____ ____ ____ you?
3 So what ____ ____ ____ ____ ?
4 ____ ____ ____ lot of money.
5 Did you have ____ ____ ____ ____ ?
6 The manager ____ ____ ____ ____ supermarket.

4 Look at the lists.

a Match the verbs with the correct items.
(Some go with more than one.)

want	trees
offer	to open the supermarket
refuse	£125,000
invite	holiday
add	to stay in her home
plant	to build a car park

b Make complete sentences.

EXAMPLE
Sainsbury's wanted to build a car park.

c 9.3 Listen again and check your ideas.

5 Work with a partner. One person is the manager of Sainsbury's, the other is the reporter. Roleplay the interview.

6 Write a newspaper article about the story. Use your answers to exercises 2 and 4.

_____ *lives at* _____ *Cottage. Two years ago ...*

Pronunciation
/ʊ/, /uː/; *-ed* endings

1 The sounds /ʊ/ and /uː/

a 9.4 Listen and repeat the sounds and the words.

/ʊ/	/uː/
could	*through*
put	*June*

b Write these words in the correct column. Compare your ideas with a partner.

look	fruit	sugar	school	blue	took
would	book	food	good	soon	supermarket

c 9.5 Listen, check, and repeat.

d Say these sentences.
1 The cook put too much sugar in the food.
2 In June I took some fruit to school.
3 You look good in blue.
4 The two cookbooks are in the front room.

2 *-ed* endings

We can pronounce the past tense *-ed* in three ways.

a 9.6 Listen. Match the verbs and the endings.

played returned	/t/
finished looked	/ɪd/
ended waited	/d/

b Which ending do we use after
- a vowel sound or a voiced consonant? _____
- a voiceless consonant? _____
- *-t* and *-d*? _____

c Write the verbs in the correct column.

liked	started	travelled	closed
stayed	jumped	lifted	accepted
cleaned	added	needed	tried
washed	stopped	pronounced	invited

/d/	/t/	/ɪd/

d Compare your ideas with a partner.

e 9.7 Listen, check, and repeat.

➤ Check the rules for the pronunciation of *-ed* endings in **Grammar Reference 9.1**.

10 Travel

Grammar
The past simple tense: irregular verbs

Grammar in use

1 Look at the postcard.
  1 Who is it to?
  2 Who is it from?
  3 Where is he?

2 Read the postcard. Are these sentences *True* (✓) or *False* (✗)?
  1 ☐ Matt arrived in Peru yesterday.
  2 ☐ He travelled by bus.
  3 ☐ He was ill for two days.
  4 ☐ Matt went to Machu Picchu three days ago.
  5 ☐ He didn't take a camera with him.
  6 ☐ He sent his parents a postcard from Colombia.

Las ruinas de Machu Picchu.
The ruins of Machu Picchu.

Dear Mum and Dad,
   Well, here I am in Peru on our South American tour. We got to Lima five days ago. We had a good journey. It took three days by bus, but we saw lots of things on the way. We didn't do much for the first two days, as a couple of the other guys were ill. We spent most of the time on the beach. (They're OK now!) On Wednesday we came up to the mountains, and yesterday we went to the old Inca city of Machu Picchu and did some sightseeing. It was fantastic! We didn't have a lot of time there, but we saw everything and I took lots of photos.
   Hope you're well. Did you get my card from Colombia?
        Love
            Matt
PS We're off to Bolivia tomorrow!

Mr and Mrs J Halstead
56 Ashton Drive
Portsmouth
PO5 7BU
Reino Unido

Rules

1 A lot of common verbs in English have an irregular past tense form.

a Find the past tenses of these verbs in the postcard.

do _____

see _____

get _____

spend _____

go _____

take _____

have _____

b Look at the list of irregular verbs on p127.
 1 Which of these verbs are irregular?
 2 What are the past forms?

break	find	win	buy
cook	dance	swim	drink
drive	eat	enjoy	arrive
hold	work	speak	know
like	live	think	make
meet	offer	come	open
say	start	want	write

2 How do we make negatives and questions with irregular verbs?

a Complete these sentences from the postcard.

We _____ a good journey.

We _____ a lot of time.

We _____ to Lima five days ago.

_____ you _____ my card from Colombia?

b Complete these sentences with the correct form of the regular verb *visit*.

positive We _____ Peru last year.

negative We _____ _____ Machu Picchu.

question _____ you _____ Lima?

c Now complete the sentences again with the verb *go*.

positive We _____ to Peru last year.

negative We _____ _____ to Machu Picchu.

question _____ you _____ to Lima?

d Compare the sentences with *visit* and *go*. What form of the verbs do we use in negatives and questions?

e Are the rules for negatives and questions the same for regular and irregular verbs?

➤ Check the rules for the past simple tense: irregular verbs in **Grammar Reference 10.1**.

Practice

1 Later on the tour Matt telephoned his parents.

a Complete the conversation. Put the verbs in the box into the past simple tense. (Some are used more than once.)

leave	be	go back	lose	happen	visit	do
have	find	not have	spend	not find	not be	get

Matt Hi, Dad.

Father Hello, Matt. How are you?

Matt I'm fine, thanks. We're in Bolivia now.

Father _____ you _____ a good time in Peru?

Matt Yes, we _____ .

Father We _____ your postcard last week. How long _____ you _____ there?

Matt We _____ there for about three weeks.

Father What _____ you _____ ?

Matt Oh, we _____ lots of places.

Father _____ you _____ good places to stay?

Matt Yes, we _____ _____ any problems. But guess what. I _____ my wallet.

Father Oh no! How _____ that _____ ?

Matt I _____ it on the beach.

Father _____ you _____ it again?

Matt No, I _____ . We _____ to look for it, but we _____ _____ it. But it _____ OK. There _____ much in it. My passport and tickets and money _____ all at the hotel …

b Compare your ideas with a partner.

c 📼 *10.1* Listen and check.

2 You are on holiday. Look at the pictures. Four of these things played a part in your first week. Write a postcard to a friend and describe your holiday.

Vocabulary
Travel

1 Complete the words with the endings in the box. Use a dictionary to help you.

gle	ket	port	tel	sa
ley	senger	form	case	ght
tion	gage	ney	ing pass	
port	at	turn	ler's cheques	

1 tic_____
2 pass_____
3 suit_____
4 ho_____
5 lug_____
6 sin_____
7 re_____
8 vi_____
9 jour_____
10 fli_____
11 travel_____
12 air_____
13 sta_____
14 plat_____
15 board_____
16 se_____
17 pas_____
18 trol_____

2 Complete these sentences with words from exercise 1.

1 You have to buy a _____ for the train.
2 If you want to come back you need a _____ ticket.
3 Trains stop at a _____ .
4 When you wait for a train, you stand on the _____ .
5 You sit on a _____ .
6 At airports you often have to show your _____ .
7 To visit some countries you need a _____ .
8 You pack a _____ .
9 Your _____ is all your bags and suitcases.
10 You check in for a _____ at an airport.
11 You check into and check out of a _____ .
12 At an airport you put your luggage on a _____ .

3 What happens when you go on holiday? Describe the process.

EXAMPLE

First you go to a travel agent's. You choose a holiday. You talk to the travel agent. You book …

Reading and writing
Torquay? But I said Turkey!

1 Look at the first paragraph.
1 What is the woman's name?
2 Where is she from?
3 Where does she work?
4 Where was she last week?
5 Where did she want to fly to?

2 Read the whole story and answer the questions.
1 What happened to the woman?
2 Why did it happen?
3 How did she feel about it afterwards?

TORQUAY?
But I said
TURKEY!

KUMIKO TSUCHIDA is a Japanese professor and she works in Turkey at Istanbul University. Last week she took a short holiday in London. She had a good time, and after a few days she packed her suitcase, checked out of the hotel, and set off to catch her flight back to Istanbul.

At Paddington station she couldn't find the train to the airport, so she asked a railway guard. Mrs Tsuchida doesn't speak very much English, and when she said 'Turkey', the guard thought that she said 'Torquay', a seaside town in south-west England. So he directed her to the platform for the 8.15 train to Torquay.

Mrs Tsuchida got on the train and found a seat. The journey seemed very long, but when she asked the other passengers 'Turkey?' they all said that yes, she was on the right train for Torquay.

She arrived in the seaside town just after midnight, but when she got off the train, of

UNITED KINGDOM

Torq

3 **Read the story again. Number these events in the correct order.**

- [ ] She travelled to Heathrow airport.
- [ ] She caught a flight to Istanbul.
- [ ] She got on the train.
- [ ] She went to Paddington station.
- [ ] The police found her.
- [ ] A railway guard directed her to the Torquay train.
- [ ] She spoke to a reporter.
- [ ] The police phoned the Japanese embassy.
- [ ] She spent a few days in London.
- [1] She left Turkey.
- [ ] She arrived in Torquay.

4 **Write about something that happened to you on a journey or a holiday.**

Language focus: Past tenses

a Underline all the past tense verbs in the story.

b Write the infinitive of the verbs. Which ones are irregular?

Vocabulary file: Transport

a Match the words and the pictures.

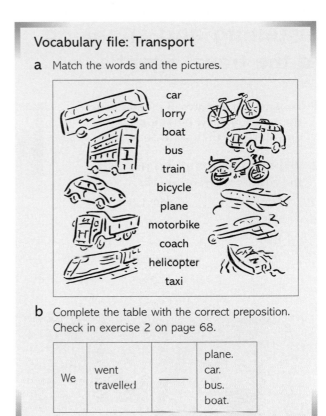

car
lorry
boat
bus
train
bicycle
plane
motorbike
coach
helicopter
taxi

b Complete the table with the correct preposition. Check in exercise 2 on page 68.

We	went travelled	———	plane. car. bus. boat.

Istanbul

Ankara

TURKEY

don

course, she didn't recognize anything. She didn't know where she was. She didn't have any English money and she was very frightened.

Two hours later, the police found her. They provided a bed for her for the night and the next morning they phoned the Japanese embassy. The embassy sorted out the problem. Then Mrs Tsuchida got the train back to London, took a taxi to Heathrow airport, and caught another flight to Istanbul.

Before she left, she spoke to our reporter through an interpreter. 'I said "Turkey, Turkey", but people didn't understand my pronunciation and they thought I said "Torquay". But I enjoyed my visit and English people are very helpful and kind.'

Listening and speaking
At the travel agent's

1 Look at the pictures of customers at the travel agency. What kind of trips do you think they want to book?

2 🎞 *10.2* Listen. Tick (✓) the places the customers want to visit.

☐ Portugal   ☐ Sydney
☐ Singapore   ☐ Moscow
☐ Italy   ☐ Brazil
☐ the USA   ☐ South Africa

3 🎞 *10.2* Listen again and complete the chart.

	1	2	3
Where?			
When?			
How long?			
How many people?			
Transport?			
Accommodation?			

4 **What other information can you remember about each customer?**

a Write down your ideas.

b Compare your ideas with a partner.

c 🔊 *10.2* Listen again and check.

Conversation pieces: Making travel arrangements

a Match the two parts of the sentences. (Some can go with more than one part.)

When do you want	accommodation?
I'd like a hotel	by train.
Do you need	the flight?
Whereabouts	to travel?
How many people	to go?
We'd like to go	about two weeks there.
Is it	to go for?
How would you like	in Australia?
We'd like to book	near the centre.
How long do you want	for two people?
How long is	is it for?
We want to spend	a trip to Italy.

b Which things do the customers say? Which things does the travel agent say?

c Complete the questions with these words.

economy	like	direct	fly	over	want

Do you _____	to _____ ?
	to fly _____ ?
Would you _____	to stop _____ on the way?
	to fly business class or _____ ?

d Check your ideas in tapescript 10.2.

---

5 **Work with a partner. Make new conversations at the travel agent's.**

a Look at the chart in exercise 3. Decide on the details of your trip.

b Roleplay the conversations.

➤ See **Functional Language: Travel arrangements** p114.

Pronunciation
/æ/, /eɪ/; intonation

1 **The sounds /æ/ and /eɪ/**

a Write these words in the correct column.

cake	rain	came	say
apple	plane	lemonade	back
play	bank	game	wait
fat	stay	balcony	jazz
man	ran	actor	bad

/æ/	/eɪ/
apple	cake

b 🔊 *10.3* Listen, check, and repeat.

c Match the spellings and the sounds.

	/æ/	/eɪ/
ai		
a + one consonant (except *y*)		
a + *y*		
a + two consonants		
a + one consonant + *e*		

2 **Intonation: statements and Yes / No questions**

a 🔊 *10.4* Listen to these sentences. Which one goes up at the end?
statement *We went to Turkey.*
question *Did you like it?*

b 🔊 *10.5* Listen and repeat these sentences.

1 Was the weather nice?

2 We visited an old town.

3 Did you go by plane?

4 It rained for two weeks.

5 They travelled by plane.

6 Did you stay with friends?

c 🔊 *10.5* Listen again and draw the intonation curves.

EXAMPLES

Was the weather nice?

We visited an old town.

d Compare your ideas with a partner. Practise saying the sentences.

Extension Units 9 and 10

Language check

General review

1 Correct the sentences. Each sentence has one mistake.

1 We goed to Prague for a holiday.
2 Did you saw the match last night?
3 I didn't wrote any postcards.
4 Did you were away at the weekend?
5 Mrs Cootes sliped on the wet ground.
6 I cryed when they left.
7 Took you a lot of photographs?
8 We didn't wanted to go to the park.
9 When arrived the plane?
10 **A** Did you like film?
   B Yes, we liked.
11 They travelled in plane.
12 The shop closed ago ten minutes.

Past simple

2 Bill and Carla were on holiday last week. Carla is talking about it. Put the verbs in brackets into the past simple tense.

1 Bill _lost_ (lose) our camera.
2 We _stayed_ (stay) in a good hotel.
3 I _bought_ (buy) a lot of souvenirs.
4 We _sent_ (send) postcards to all our friends.
5 I _tried_ (try) all the local food.
6 We _met_ (meet) some interesting people.
7 They _showed_ (show) us some good restaurants.
8 We really _liked_ (like) the beach.
9 We _spent_ (spend) a lot of time there.
10 We _came_ (come) back last Sunday.

Past simple negative

3 These things didn't happen on the holiday. Make the sentences negative.

1 They hired a car.
2 They went to Rome.
3 Bill played golf.
4 They found their camera.
5 Carla phoned her parents.
6 They visited lots of museums.
7 They had good weather all the time.
8 They did a lot of sightseeing.

Past simple questions

4 Joe and Esther went on a day out last week. Joe is talking to his friend Tony. Write Tony's questions.

have a good time?	Where / go?	ill?
What / do?	good?	What / see?
have a day off work yesterday?		

Tony _did you have a day off work yesterd_

Joe Yes, I did.

Tony _Were you ill ?_

Joe No, I wasn't. I had a day out with Esther.

Tony _did you go? ?_

Joe We went to London.

Tony _did you have a good time?_

Joe Yes, it was great.

Tony _what did you do ?_

Joe We went shopping and then in the evening we went to the theatre.

Tony _what did you see ?_

Joe We saw *Cats*.

Tony _was it good_

Joe It was fantastic!

Conversations _Hom Work_

5 Write the questions to complete the conversation.

Travel agent Hello. _Can I help you_ ?

Customer I'd like to book a flight to Egypt, please.

Travel agent _where about in Egept_ ?

Customer Cairo.

Travel agent _When do you go_ ?

Customer In September, please.

Travel agent _How long do want to stay_ ?

Customer About ten days.

Travel agent _How many people_ ?

Customer It's for two people. Myself and my wife.

Travel agent _Do you need accommodation_

Customer No, thank you. We've got friends out there.

Vocabulary

6 Look at the Wordlist for Units 9 and 10.
Make questions and answers about ten words.

EXAMPLE
*A How do you say **pasaporte** in English?*
B Passport.

Extra!
'Where did you go on holiday?'

1 🔲 **Listen to the conversations. Which places did the people visit?**

2 **Look at the chart.**

a 🔲 Listen and complete the chart.

b 🔲 Listen again and check your ideas.

	Julia	David
Where?		
How long?		
Weather?		
Transport?		
Journey time?		
Stay?		
Do?		
Get back?		

3 **Describe the two holidays.**

a Complete this description of Julia's holiday.
Julia and her husband went to … for a week. It rained … They went by … and the journey took … They stayed … While they were there they … They got back …

b Describe David's holiday.

4 **Look at the chart in exercise 2.**

a What questions did the speakers ask to get the information?

b Check your ideas in the tapescript on p124.

c What other questions could you ask about someone's holiday?

5 **Work in pairs. Use the questions. Ask your partner about his / her last holiday (real or imaginary).**

11 Fashion

Grammar
The present continuous tense

Grammar in use

1 Choose the second parts of the conversations.
Match A, B, and C to the correct pictures.

> Hi, Tim. What are you watching?

1

> Oh, hi, Zach. It's the Liverpool match. They're playing Arsenal.

> Hello, Suzanne. What are you doing these days?

2

> I'm studying chemistry at university, Uncle George.

> Hi, Bella.

3

> Hello, Cindy. Welcome to the party. Is it still raining?

> Yes, it is. Paul's just coming.

A
> What's he doing?

> He's parking the car.

B
> Are you enjoying it?

> Yes, I am. It's great!

C
> Are they winning?

> No, they aren't. They're losing 3–1 at the moment, and they aren't playing very well, either.

2 Complete these sentences with a subject.
1 _He/sh_ is having a party.
2 _She_ is studying chemistry.
3 _They_ are arriving at the party.
4 _It_ is raining.
5 _they_ aren't winning.
6 _He_ is talking to his niece.
7 _He_ is watching TV.

Rules

1 Look at these sentences.
I'm studying chemistry.
He's parking the car.
They're playing Arsenal.

a The verbs are in the present continuous tense.
This describes what is happening now or for a
limited period.

b Find more examples of the present continuous in
the conversations.

c How do we make the present continuous tense?
What two parts does it have? Which part changes
with different subjects?

2 Find these verbs in the conversation.
lose   win

a What happens to them in the *-ing* form?

b Make the *-ing* forms of these verbs.

sit	stand	stop	do	wear	take
smile	put	grab	hold	arrive	write

3 Complete this sentence from the conversations.

They ~~weren't~~ *playing very well, either.*

a Which part changes to show the negative form?

b Put the verbs in brackets into the negative form of the present continuous.

1 I _*am*_ (wear) my new coat.

2 It _*is*_ (rain).

3 We _*are*_ (enjoy) the match.

4 Find two questions in the conversations.

a How do we make questions in the present continuous?

b Turn these statements into questions and complete the short answers.

Tim is watching TV.

A _____ ?

B Yes, he _____ .

Liverpool are winning.

_____ ?

B No, they _____ .

➤ Check the rules for the present continuous tense in **Grammar Reference 11.1**.

Practice

1 Look at the pictures again. Say who is doing each thing.

EXAMPLE
talk about the weather
Bella and Cindy are talking about the weather.

1 wear a dress
2 hold something
3 take off his jacket
4 park the car
5 sit down
6 wear a tie
7 win
8 carry an umbrella
9 watch television
10 wear a hat

2 Are these sentences *True* (✓) or *False* (✗)? Correct the ones that are false.

EXAMPLE

☒ George is talking to Cindy.
George isn't talking to Cindy. He's talking to Suzanne.

1 ☒ Tim is looking at some photos.
2 ☑ Zach is arriving home.
3 ☒ Paul and Cindy are leaving the party.
4 ☑ Paul is paying the taxi driver.
5 ☑ Suzanne is studying chemistry.
6 ☒ George is sitting down.
7 ☒ Bella is wearing jeans.

3 Work in pairs.
A Mime an activity.
B Guess what A is doing.

EXAMPLE
B Are you typing?
A No, I'm not.
B Are you playing the piano?
A Yes, I am.

4 Complete these conversations. Put the verbs in brackets into the present continuous.

1 **A** _____ you _____ (go out)?
B Yes, we _____ . We _____ (go) to the cinema.
A Well, it _____ (rain).
B It's OK. We _____ (take) a taxi.
It _____ (wait) outside now.

2 **A** _____ you _____ (enjoy) the party?
B Yes, I _____ . Where's Justin?
A He's in the kitchen. He _____ (make) some coffee. Is Michelle here?
B Yes. She _____ (sit) over there with Ben.

Vocabulary
Clothes

1 **Look at the pictures. Which clothes can you name?**

Penny   Michael

Adam   Paulette

Winston   Judy

2 **Read the descriptions.**

Michael and Penny are going to a wedding. Penny is wearing a blue dress and a white hat and gloves. Her shoes are black and she's wearing tights. She's carrying a bag. Michael is wearing a brown suit with a white shirt and a red tie. His shoes are brown. He's carrying a coat.

Adam is wearing a green T-shirt, black shorts, white socks, and black and white trainers. He's got a baseball cap on his head. Paulette is wearing a red skirt with a white top and purple boots.

Winston is wearing a blue shirt with a jumper and trousers. His jumper is yellow and his trousers are brown. He's carrying a blue jacket. Judy is wearing jeans and an orange sweatshirt.

a Label the pictures with these words.

shirt	T-shirt	skirt	coat	shoes
gloves	trousers	jeans	top	tights
socks	trainers	suit	tie	shorts
jacket	jumper	dress	hat	sweatshirt
bag	boots	baseball cap		

b Compare your ideas with a partner.

3 **Look at this sentence.**
His jumper is yellow and his trousers are brown.

a What do you notice about the word *trousers*?

b Some names of clothes are always plural. Find some more words like this.

c Complete the sentences.
   EXAMPLE
   Michael's suit is brown.
   1 Adam's _____ black.
   2 Paulette's _____ red.
   3 Judy's _____ blue.
   4 Penny's _____ blue.
   5 Winston's _____ brown.

4 **What are you wearing today?**
Describe your clothes.

5 **Work with a partner.**
   A Describe what someone in the class is wearing, or use the pictures on p76.
   B Say who it is.

Reading and writing
A model pupil

1 Look at the pictures and the headline.
1 What is the girl's name?
2 Where is she in the pictures?
3 What do you think the article is about?

2 Read the article. Who or what are these?
- Stacey Thomas
- Westin High
- *Flair*
- Zoe Carson
- Barbara Adams
- Ella Marie

3 Read the text again. Put these items in the correct column.

appear at a fashion show	meet new people
do her homework	walk along the catwalk
stay at a hotel	wear the latest fashions
walk across the playground	go to parties
meet her friends	live at home
nobody / look at her ·	wear a uniform
hundreds of people / watch her	
go to school	

Tamara's normal life	This week

4 What do you think of Tamara's situation?

Language focus: Present simple and present continuous

a Complete these sentences from the text.
Tamara _____ the school uniform.
She _____ the latest fashions.

b What are the two tenses?

c Which tense describes
- something that happens regularly or every day?
- something that is happening now or at the moment?

d Look at the table in exercise 3. Compare Tamara's normal life with this week.

EXAMPLE
Tamara normally goes to school, but this week she's appearing at a fashion show.

➤ Check the rules for the present simple and present continuous in **Grammar Reference 11.2**.

5 Imagine you are doing exactly what you'd like to do today. Write a paragraph. Compare what you normally do with what you're doing today.

Tamara's a model pupil

Tamara Adams is fifteen years old. She normally catches the bus to school at 8.30. She meets her best friend, Stacey Thomas, at the bus stop. Like all the other girls at Westin High School, Tamara wears the school uniform – a green skirt and a white blouse, with green socks, a green tie, and a blue jacket. When she comes home in the evening, she does her homework and watches TV.

But this week Tamara isn't going to school. She isn't living at home. She's staying at an expensive London hotel. And she definitely isn't wearing her school uniform. She's wearing the latest fashions.

Six months ago Tamara won a competition in *Flair* magazine. The prize was to be a model in a top fashion show this week. So now it's 11 o'clock on Wednesday morning. At this time Tamara usually walks across the school playground to her next lesson. Nobody looks at her. She's just another girl with her friends. But this week things are different. She isn't walking across the playground. She's walking along the catwalk at the London Clothes Show. Hundreds of people are watching her and cameras are flashing.

Tamara's mother, Barbara, is here, too. At the moment she's sitting with Zoe Carson from the Ella Marie modelling agency. Zoe: 'I think Tamara has got a great future as a model. Today models are like film stars. They have to work hard, but they can earn millions.'

What does Tamara think? 'Well, I'm enjoying this week. I'm meeting lots of new people and there are parties every night. I've got my GCSE exams in June and I'm working hard for them, but after that, well, I think I'd really like to be a model.'

Barbara is worried: 'Tamara's only 15 years old, and yesterday Ella Marie offered her a contract for £50,000 a year. That's a lot of money. But things can change so quickly. This year you're number one and next year nobody wants you. But nobody can take your education away from you.'

Listening and speaking
In a clothes shop

1 **Look at the pictures.**
  1 Who are the people?
  2 Where are they?
  3 What are they doing?

2 📼 *11.1* **Listen to the conversations.
What does each person buy?**

3 📼 *11.1* **Listen again and complete the chart.**

	1	2	3
What do they buy?			
What size do they ask for?			
How much does each thing cost?			
What does each person pay?			
How do they pay?			

Language focus: Words with no singular

a Look back at the **Vocabulary** section on p78. What does it say about words like *trousers* and *shorts*?

b Complete these conversations.
  A How much _____ _____ trousers?
  B _____ £47.50.
  A Can I try _____ on?
  B Yes, of course.

  A How much _____ _____ skirt?
  B _____ £34.
  A Can I try _____ on?
  B Yes, of course.

c Work with a partner. Make similar conversations for these things.
  ● shorts £15.00
  ● top £18.50
  ● jeans £43.90
  ● jacket £92.00

Conversation pieces: Buying clothes

a 🔲 *11.1* Listen to the third conversation again and complete the gaps.

Assistant Can I _____ you?

Customer Yes. How _____ is this tracksuit?

Assistant It's £63.20.

Customer Have you got it in a _____ size?

Assistant Yes, _____ you are. Medium.

Customer Thank you. Where can I _____ it on?

Assistant The _____ are over there, next to the jeans.

Customer Thank you.

Assistant _____ is it?

Customer It's _____ , thanks. I'll _____ it.

Assistant Do you want _____ else?

Customer Yes, _____ I have this cap?

Assistant That's £68.70 then, please.

Customer Do you _____ credit cards?

Assistant Certainly. Could you _____ here, please? There you are. That's your copy.

Customer Thank you. Goodbye.

Assistant Goodbye.

b Look at this sentence. How can you say the same thing in another way?
Do you take credit cards?

c Check your answers in tapescript 11.1.

d Work with a partner. Read the conversations.

4 **Work with a partner. Make new conversations for these things.**
- jacket / £75 / size 40 / tie / £15
- shoes / £23 / size 7 / socks / £4.99
- shorts / £14.90 / medium / bag / £6.50
- sweatshirt / £24 / extra large / nothing else

Pronunciation
/ɒ/, /əʊ/; intonation

1 The sounds /ɒ/ and /əʊ/

a 🔲 *11.2* Listen. Which pair do you hear?
1 not   note
2 note   not

b Write these words with *coffee* or *toast*.

coffee	photo	dog	want	go
toast	no	over	ago	what
old	box	model	wash	long
stop	OK	nose	both	open

/ɒ/	/əʊ/
coffee	*toast*

c Compare your ideas with a partner.

d 🔲 *11.3* Listen, check, and repeat.

e Say these sentences. How many /ɒ/ and /əʊ/ sounds are there in each sentence?

	/ɒ/	/əʊ/
1 Go to the postbox opposite the post office.	☐	☐
2 I don't want to go to the doctor's.	☐	☐
3 There are lots of old photos in the box.	☐	☐
4 The shop's going to close in October.	☐	☐
5 I hope you got my postcard.	☐	☐

2 Intonation: *Wh-* questions

We saw in Unit 10 that Yes / No questions have rising intonation.

a 🔲 *11.4* Listen to these *Wh-* questions. Does the intonation rise or fall?
What are you doing?
How old are you?

b Look at these questions. Draw the intonation curves.

1 Are you leaving now?

2 What do you do?

3 Where are you going?

4 Is Bill here?

5 Do you like this dress?

6 How much are these shoes?

c Compare your ideas with a partner. Practise saying the sentences.

d 🔲 *11.5* Listen, check, and repeat.

12 Health

Grammar
Comparatives and superlatives

Grammar in use

1 Look at the pictures.
1 What kind of place is it?
2 What are the people in the pictures doing?
3 Why do people go to these places?
4 Have you ever been to a place like this? Would you like to go?

2 Read the text. Which ideas does the article use to recommend the place?
1 You can get fitter.
2 You can lose weight.
3 Health farms are becoming very popular.
4 Health farms are cheaper than other hotels.
5 The food is very good.
6 You feel a lot better afterwards.
7 People are healthier in winter.
8 The prices are lower for winter weekends.
9 Henley Manor isn't the most expensive health farm in the country.

Rules

1 This table shows the comparative and superlative of some adjectives.

a Find the missing forms in the text. Complete the table.

adjective	comparative	superlative
young	younger	the youngest
cold	colder	_____
large	larger	_____
fit	_____	the fittest
healthy	_____	the healthiest
relaxed	_____	the most relaxed
expensive	more expensive	_____

b Compare the comparatives and superlatives with your language. What differences are there?

HEALTH FARMS

Do you want to be fitter and healthier? Would you like to look younger? Do you want to feel more relaxed? Then try a few days at a health farm. Health farms are becoming one of the most popular places for a short break. I went to Henley Manor for a weekend. It's the largest health farm in the country but it isn't the most expensive. After two days of exercise and massage I felt ten times better. But the best thing for me was the food. It was all very healthy, of course, but it was excellent, too!

Winter breaks

If you're looking for something a bit cheaper, try a winter break. Winter is the darkest and the coldest time of the year, and it can also be the worst time for your body. We all eat too much and we don't take enough exercise. A lot of health farms offer lower prices Monday to Friday from November to March.

2 How do we make comparatives and superlatives?

a Find an example in the table for this general rule.

> We add *-er* to make the comparative and *the* + *-est* to make the superlative.
> EXAMPLE
>
> _____ _____ _____

b Look at the table. Complete these rules.

> 1 When the adjective ends in *-e*, we add _____ for the comparative and _____ for the superlative.
> 2 When the adjective has a short vowel and one consonant we _____ the consonant.
> 3 When the adjective ends in *-y* we change *-y* to _____ .
> 4 When the adjective has two or more syllables (except when the second syllable is *-y*) we use _____ to make the comparative and _____ to make the superlative.

c Write the comparative and superlative of these adjectives.

long _____ _____
nice _____ _____
slim _____ _____
happy _____ _____
difficult _____ _____

3 The comparative and superlative of *good, bad,* and *far* are irregular. Find the missing words in the text.

good _____ _____
bad worse _____
far further the furthest

4 Look at exercise 2 on p 82.

a Complete these sentences.
Health farms are cheaper _____ other hotels.
It isn't the most expensive health farm _____ the country.

b Compare the sentences with your language.

➤ Check the rules for comparative and superlative adjectives in **Grammar Reference 12.1**.

Practice

1 Look at the conversation.

a Put the adjectives in brackets into the comparative form.

Interviewer Why did you decide to go to a health farm?
Guest I was _____ (fat) and _____ (heavy) than I wanted to be.
Interviewer Why did you choose Henley Manor? Was it _____ (cheap) than other places?
Guest No, in fact it was _____ (expensive) than some other places, but it was _____ (near) home, so it was _____ (convenient).
Interviewer What was it like?
Guest Well, it was _____ (difficult) than I expected. In fact after two days I felt _____ (bad) than before, but after that things became _____ (easy).
Interviewer And how do you feel now?
Guest I feel a lot _____ (happy). I'm _____ (slim) and I feel ten years _____ (young)! I eat _____ (healthy) food now, and my lifestyle is _____ (slow) and _____ (relaxed). I go to bed _____ (early) and I sleep _____ (good).

b 🔊 *12.1* Listen and check your answers.

2 Compare these things. Write two sentences for each.
- winter and summer
- you and your best friend
- your mother and your father
- yourself now and ten years ago
- your last two holidays
- the last two films that you saw
- Units 10 and 11 in this book

3 Work in groups of four. Use the superlatives of the adjectives to describe the people in your group.

EXAMPLES
Johann is the tallest person in our group.
Sasha is the shortest.
1 tall / short
2 large / small hands
3 long / short hair
4 dark / fair hair
5 get up / early / late
6 live / far from / near the school
7 good / bad marks in the last test
8 heavy / light bag
9 interesting hobby

Vocabulary
Parts of the body

1 **Look at the picture. How many parts of the body can you name?**

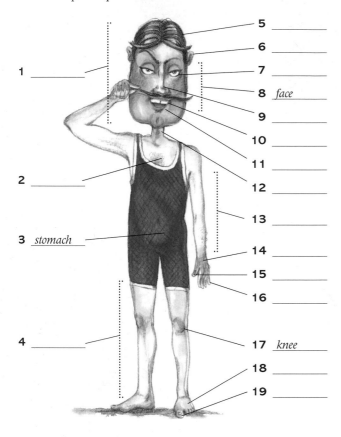

1 _____
2 _____
3 _stomach_
4 _____

5 _____
6 _____
7 _____
8 _face_
9 _____
10 _____
11 _____
12 _____
13 _____
14 _____
15 _____
16 _____
17 _knee_
18 _____
19 _____

2 **Read the clues and label the picture.**

- You have got two arms and two legs. Your legs are longer than your arms.
- At the end of each arm is a hand and on each hand you've got four fingers and a thumb.
- At the end of your legs are your feet. Each foot has got five toes.
- Your chest is above your stomach. Your neck is between your chest and your head.
- There is an ear on each side of your head. You hear with your ears. There is hair on top of your head.
- The front of your head is face. You have got two eyes. You see with them. You have a nose and a mouth. You eat and speak with your mouth. Inside your mouth you have got teeth and a tongue. Your teeth are white.

3 **Two of the words have an irregular plural.**
1 What is the plural of _foot_?
2 What do you think the singular of _teeth_ is?

Reading and writing
Aliens

1 **Some people believe that creatures from other planets visit the Earth. What do you think?**

2 **Look at the pictures. What is happening?**

3 **Look quickly at the text.**
1 What is the woman's name?
2 When did the story happen?

4 **Read the story. Number the pictures in the correct order.**

5 **Answer the questions.**
1 Why did Anna wake up?
2 How did the creatures get Anna into the spaceship?
3 What was strange about the creatures' hands?
4 What was different about the fourth creature?
5 What did the creatures do to Anna?
6 Did she feel any pain?
7 How did Anna know that it wasn't a dream?
8 What is interesting about David E. Jacobs' work?

6 **Write the story from the creatures' point of view.**
- How did you get to the garden?
- What did you want to do?
- How did you get the woman?
- What did she look like to you?
- What did you do with her? Why?
- What did you do afterwards?

Vocabulary file: Synonyms and adjectives

a Find words or expressions in the text to match these definitions.
- in the morning
- very large
- A car has four of these.
- the opposite of _push_
- You think these.
- She wanted to sleep.
- the opposite of _woke up_
- You see yourself in this.

b What are described in the text by these adjectives?

strange	large	dirty	small	amazing
bright	taller	tired	fairer	thinner	huge

Are we alone in the universe?

Or is there life on other planets? Do creatures from space visit the Earth? Many people believe that they do. Anna Clarke is one of those people. This is her story.

It happened on 21 November 1990. Anna Clarke suddenly woke up. It was 3.15 a.m. She could see a bright light outside. She got up, walked to the window, and looked out. There was a strange object like a huge wheel above the garden. At the centre of the wheel there was a bright white light. The light started to move closer. Anna wanted to run away, but she couldn't move. Then she heard a voice inside her head. It said: 'Don't worry. Follow the light.' The light pulled her downstairs and through the front door. When she was outside, the light pulled her up into the wheel.

Three small brown creatures appeared. They were naked. Their arms and legs were thinner than a person's. On each hand there were only three fingers and no thumb. Their heads were large with a small nose and mouth, and they had huge, black eyes. The creatures took Anna to a larger room and put her on a kind of table.

Another creature came into the room. It was taller and fairer than the others. The creature pushed something into Anna's neck below her right ear. Anna looked into the creature's eyes and she didn't feel any pain. Something seemed to pull her thoughts from her head. She felt very tired and she fell asleep.

When she woke up, she was in her bedroom again and it was morning. She remembered the light and the creatures. She thought it was just a dream. But then she noticed that her feet were dirty, and when she looked in the mirror she saw a small cut on her neck just below her right ear.

Do you believe Anna's story? Perhaps you do, perhaps you don't. However, many people believe that similar things happened to them. David E. Jacobs, an American writer, studied sixty of these stories. The most amazing thing about the stories was that the sixty people didn't know each other, but they all described the same creatures. How do you feel about Anna's story now?

Extension Units 11 and 12

Language check

The present continuous tense

1 Complete the conversations. Put the verbs into the present continuous tense.

go	look for	wear

A Why _____ John _____ a suit and tie?
B He _____ for a job interview.
A Oh, _____ he _____ a new job?
B Yes, he _____ .

rain	put on	get	not go out

A Bye.
B I _____ .
A Well, why _____ you _____ your coat?
B I _____ something from the car and it _____ .

stay	enjoy

A My parents are on holiday in Scotland this week.
B Oh, where _____ they _____ ?
A In Glasgow. They phoned yesterday.
B _____ they _____ it?
A No, they _____ . The weather's terrible.

The present continuous and the present simple

2 Choose the correct form of the verbs.
1 *Do you wear* / *Are you wearing* a suit every day?
2 **A** What *do you do?* / *are you doing?*
  B I'm an engineer.
3 **A** Hello. Can I speak to Martin, please?
  B No, I'm afraid he *has* / *'s having* a shower.
4 It *rains* / *is raining* today.
5 How often *do you play* / *are you playing* tennis?
6 **A** Where's Celia?
  B She *spends* / *'s spending* the weekend at a health farm.
7 **A** Are you ready?
  B Yes. Just a minute. I *look* / *'m looking* for the tickets.
8 We *usually go out* / *are usually going out* on Fridays.
9 **A** What *do you watch?* / *are you watching?*
  B A film, but I *don't enjoy* / *'m not enjoying* it.
10 **A** Are the visitors here?
  B Yes, they *wait* / *'re waiting* downstairs.

Comparisons

3 Compare the things. Use the adjectives in brackets.

1 Woolford Hall is _____ than Barton Grange, but Henley Manor is _____ .
(popular)

2 Tracey is _____ Alma, but Colleen is _____ .
(slim)

3 Ben's suitcase is _____ William's, but Andy's is _____ _____ . (heavy)

Conversations

4 Correct the mistakes. There is a mistake in each line.
1 **A** Do you like this jeans?
  B Yes, I do. How many are they?
  A It's £45.
  B Oh? The prices were more good in the other shop.

2 **A** These shorts is nice.
  B Yes, I like it, too.
  A Excuse me. Have you got these shorts on a size 10?
  C No, I'm afraid we haven't got.

3 **A** What's matter?
  B I have thirsty.
  A Well, you should have something drink.
  B Yes. Do you like a drink, too?

Vocabulary

5 Look at the Wordlist for Units 11 and 12.
Make ten sentences with words from the **Wordlist**.
EXAMPLE
painkiller   *I take painkillers when I have a headache.*

Extra!

'I didn't feel well.'

1 🔊 Listen to the conversations. Match the subjects and the sentence endings.

	had stomach ache.
Maria	hurt his wrist.
Pedro	had a bad cold.
Anne	broke his leg
Sanjit	had toothache.
	didn't feel well.

2 🔊 Listen again.

a What did each person do?

b How do they feel now?

3 Describe what happened to each person.

a Complete this summary for Maria.

Maria wasn't at work last week, because she _____ . She had a sore throat and a _____ . She _____ to the doctor's. She just _____ . She feels _____ now.

b Write summaries for the other three people.

4 Work with a partner. Make new conversations. Use this information.

- last week / cold / stay in bed, take medicine / better now
- yesterday / very tired / have a rest / not much better
- Wednesday / hospital / slip in garden, cut hand / better, but still hurts
- weekend / stomach ache / doctor, medicine / worse now

Great balls of fire

1 Connect the words in the box that rhyme.

brain	thumbs	honey	good	baby	thrill
fine	kind	crazy	fun	mine	should
mind	funny	will	insane		

2 Now complete the song with the words. (One word is used twice.)

You shake my nerves and you rattle my _____ ,
Too much love drives a man _____ .
You broke my _____ ,
But what a _____ .
Goodness gracious! Great balls of fire.

I laughed at love 'cos I thought it was _____ ,
You came along and moved me, _____ .
I've changed my _____ ,
This world is _____ .
Goodness gracious! Great balls of fire.

Mmm, kiss me, baby.
Ooh, it feels _____ .
Hold me, baby.
I want to love you like a lover _____ .
You're _____ ,
So _____ .
I want to tell the world you're mine, mine, mine,
_____ .

I chew my nails and I twiddle my _____ ,
I'm real nervous but it sure is _____ .
Come on, _____ ,
Drive me _____ .
Goodness gracious! Great balls of fire.

3 🔊 Listen and check your answers.

13 Winners

Grammar
going to

Grammar in use

1 Look at the story.
  1 Who are the people?
  2 Why are they interested in the lottery numbers?
  3 What happens?

2 Complete these sentences with the names of the people.
  1 _____ thinks it's going to be great.
  2 _____ wants to buy a sports car.
  3 _____ doesn't want to spend the money.
  4 _____ wants to go to an expensive restaurant.
  5 _____ forgot to buy the ticket.

Rules

1 Look at these sentences from the story.

a Complete the sentences.
  I _____ buy a sports car.
  It _____ be great!
  They _____ give the lottery numbers.

b What time are the people talking about?
  ● the past
  ● the present
  ● the future

Max, Ellen, Jeff, Sarah, and Stuart work together in an office. Every week they buy a ticket for the national lottery …

Ssh. They're going to give the lottery numbers.

7, 12, 23, 35, 46, and 47

They're our numbers. I don't believe it. We're millionaires.

LATER

It's going to be great!

I'm going to buy a sports car. What are you and Ellen going to do, Max?

Oh, we aren't going to spend it. It isn't going to change our life. We …

Speak for yourself, Max. Tomorrow I'm going to have a meal in the best restaurant in town.

Are you going to buy a new car, Jeff?

Er no, I'm not. I'm not going to do anything. And I'm afraid you aren't going to do anything, either.

What? Why not?

You aren't going to believe this, but I, er I forgot to buy the ticket.

We're going to kill you.

Help!

2 **Underline more examples of** *going to* **in the story.**

a Find examples of these things.
- negatives
- questions
- short answers

b How do we make these forms?

3 **Look at these sentences.**
I'm going to save all the money.
She's going to book a holiday.
They're going to be millionaires.

a Make the sentences negative.

b Make the sentences into questions.

➤ Check the rules for *going to* in **Grammar Reference 13.1**.

Practice

1 **These people have all won the lottery. What are they going to do? Use the verbs and information in the boxes.**

fly	buy	share	travel	put	live

it all in the bank	it with her family	a horse
to New York on Concorde	in Florida	round the world

1 Robin

4 The Watsons

2 Jack and Judy

5 Harriet

3 Mr and Mrs Patel

6 Melinda

2 **Look at this interview.**

a Complete the interview. Use *going to* and the verbs in the box.

help	look for	spend	not stay
go	tell	be	not take
see	talk	buy	have to
join	make	finish	not change

DJ Hello. I'm at the *Top Band Show* here in London. An hour ago Flight won the prize for 'Best New Band of the Year'. I _____ to their singer, Kate Mahoney. First, congratulations, Kate! Tell us about the prize.

Kate Well, the most important thing is that we _____ on tour with some really famous bands next year. That _____ great!

DJ And _____ an album?

Kate We don't know yet. Our manager _____ some record companies next week.

DJ Now, you also won £5,000. How _____ it?

Kate We _____ new equipment for the band.

DJ Good idea. What about a holiday?

Kate No, we _____ a holiday – we haven't got time!

DJ _____ this prize _____ you?

Kate Yes, _____ , but it _____ things overnight. We _____ work hard to make it to the top.

DJ Now, your bass guitarist, Ryan Sweet, is still at university. _____ he _____ you on tour?

Kate No, _____ . He _____ in the band – he _____ his studies at university.

DJ _____ a new bass player?

Kate Yes, _____ . So if you can play the bass guitar, we want to hear from you!

DJ OK, Kate. Thanks very much. Now Jack Dee _____ us something about the other bands.

b 🔊 *13.1* Listen and check your answers.

Vocabulary
Phrasal verbs

1 **We saw in Unit 9 that some English verbs have more than one part.**

a With some verbs the meaning is clear from the meanings of the two parts.

EXAMPLES

The cat climbed up the tree.
I don't want to go back.
Would you like to sit down?

b Give some more examples.

2 **But with some verbs we can't tell the meaning from the meanings of the two parts.**

EXAMPLES

She is looking after the children.
I called up my friend.

3 **Complete the sentences with these verbs in the past simple tense. Use a dictionary to help you.**

come in	set off	get up	go away
take off	get on	get to	sit down
call in	put on	take up	check out of

1 I _____ at seven o'clock and _____ my dressing-gown.
2 I _____ golf five years ago.
3 We _____ at ten. We had a good journey and we _____ London at four o'clock.
4 When Sarah _____ , she _____ her coat and _____ in the living room.
5 I _____ the hotel, walked into the street, and _____ a bus.
6 A I _____ to see you on Monday evening, but you weren't in.
   B No, we _____ for a couple of days.

4 **When a verb has two parts and an object we can often put the second part of the verb after the object.**

a Look at these sentences.
I looked up the word in a dictionary.
I looked the word up in a dictionary.

b Change these sentences in the same way.
1 I'm going to switch on the radio.
2 They wanted to knock down the cottage.
3 He's going to give back the money.
4 I picked up the book.
5 Put down your pens.

Reading and writing
The Year of the Tiger

1 **Look at the pictures.**
1 Who is the young man?
2 What do you know about him?
3 What is he doing in each picture?

2 **Read the text and answer the questions.**
1 When was 'The Year of the Tiger'?
2 What happened?
3 Why was it important?

3 **Read the text again.**

a Who or what are these?
- Earl Woods
- Cypress
- Kultilda Woods
- Jeff Binns
- Eldrick Woods
- Bill Clinton
- Augusta, Georgia
- Nike

b What does the text tell us about each one?

4 **What examples does the text give to illustrate these statements?**
Everybody wanted to know him.
Tiger Woods is more important than that.

5 **What do you think?**

a What is the most interesting piece of information in the text?

b Why did the sports company offer Tiger Woods so much money?

c What other sportspeople have a big influence on their sport?

6 **Write about a famous person that you admire.**
- How did they become famous?
- Why do you admire them?

Vocabulary file: Sport

a Find all the words in the text associated with sport.

b Think of other sports. Can you add any more words? Use a dictionary to help you.

The Year of the Tiger

It was the last day of the US Masters golf tournament in Augusta, Georgia. As the slim, young man walked up to the eighteenth hole he took off his baseball cap and waved to the crowd. A few minutes later the ball fell into the hole and the crowd went wild. Tiger Woods was the new champion.

At 21 Tiger was the youngest ever champion, and he won with the best ever score. He was also the first black golfer to win a major tournament. Everybody wanted to know him. He appeared on several TV shows. The President of the United States, Bill Clinton, called him up and the sports company, Nike, offered him a contract for $40 million.

The youngest ever champion

Tiger (his real name is Eldrick) Woods was born on 30 December 1975 in Cypress, California. His mother, Kultilda, was from Thailand. His father, Earl, was an American army officer and a keen golfer. As a baby Tiger watched his father, and he started to play golf as soon as he was old enough. When he was three years old he was already a very good player, and he soon started to win tournaments. In 1991 he became the youngest ever Junior champion. In November 1996 he became a professional, and less than six months later he beat the best players in the world to win the US Masters.

He hits the ball harder and further

Some people think that Tiger is going to be even better in the future. 'He's going to win more tournaments, of course,' says golf commentator, Jeff Binns. 'But Tiger Woods is more important than that. He hits the ball harder and further than anyone else. He's young and good-looking, too, so millions of kids are going to take up golf now, and they're all going to want to play like the Tiger.'

Tiger Woods winning the US Masters

Listening and speaking
Going out

1 Look at the pictures. What are the places?

2 🔲 *13.2* Listen to the conversations. Which of the places do the people decide to go to?

3 🔲 *13.2* Listen again and answer the questions.
1 When do they want to go?
2 What do they decide to do?
3 What time do they decide to go?
4 What are they going to do first?

Conversation pieces: Making suggestions

a Complete the expressions with these words.

Why	Shall	Would	Let

_____ 's	go out.
_____ we	
_____ don't we	go out?
_____ you like to	

b Which of these ways of agreeing and disagreeing are better?

agreeing	disagreeing
That would be nice.	I'm afraid I can't.
Good idea.	No.
OK.	Sorry, I can't.
It's nice.	I'm busy.
Fine.	I don't want to.
Great.	I'm afraid I'm a
Fine idea.	bit busy.

➤ Check your ideas in **Functional Language: Making suggestions** p114.

c Look at tapescript 13.2. Read the conversations with a partner.

4 Work with a partner. Make new conversations. Use the other four pictures.

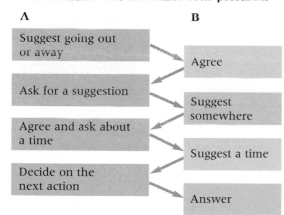

A

- Suggest going out or away
- Ask for a suggestion
- Agree and ask about a time
- Decide on the next action

B

- Agree
- Suggest somewhere
- Suggest a time
- Answer

5 Work in groups of three.

a Make plans for one of the following.
- a weekend away
- a night out
- a free afternoon

b Tell the class what you're going to do.

Pronunciation
/ʃ/, /tʃ/; how many words?

1 The sounds /ʃ/ and /tʃ/

a 🔊 13.3 Listen and repeat the sounds and the words.

/ʃ/	/tʃ/
brush	watch

b Write these words in the correct column.

conversation   cheap   teacher   sugar   cheese
professional   special   fashion   change   finish
chocolate   catch   competition   optician
moustache   wash   mushroom   station

c 🔊 13.4 Listen, check, and repeat.

d Look at the table. Which spelling usually produces each sound? Match the letters and the sounds.

	/ʃ/	/tʃ/
-tio-		
-sio-		
-cia-		
ch		
sh		

e Are there any words in the table that don't fit the rules?

f How do we pronounce these words?

headache   chemist   stomach

2 How many words?

a 🔊 13.5 Listen to the sentences. How many words are there in each sentence? (Remember: Short forms count as one word.)

EXAMPLE
1 What's he going to do?

Number
of words

1	5		6	
2			7	
3			8	
4			9	
5			10	

b Compare your ideas with a partner.

c 🔊 13.5 Listen again and write the sentences.

d Work with a partner. Practise saying the sentences.

14 Experiences

Grammar
The present perfect tense

Grammar in use

1 Look at the pictures. Have you ever done these things?

2 ▶ *14.1* **Read and listen to the conversation. Are these sentences *True* (✓) or *False* (✗)?**

1 ☐ Mark's flown in a helicopter.
2 ☐ Mark and Louise have driven a racing car.
3 ☐ Mark hasn't learned to drive.
4 ☐ Louise has driven a racing car.
5 ☐ Mark and Louise have ridden a horse.
6 ☐ Mark and Louise haven't been scuba-diving.

Mark Hey, look at this advert, Louise.
Louise What's it about?
Mark Adventure weekends. You can do all sorts of things like horse-riding, car racing, helicopter rides …
Louise Oh, that sounds exciting. Have you ever travelled in a helicopter?
Mark Yes, I have. I've flown in a helicopter twice, in fact. They're very noisy. Have you ever been in one?
Louise No, I haven't. But I've driven a racing car.
Mark Have you? I bet that was great. I haven't. Well, I haven't driven any sort of car, because I can't drive!
Louise Let's have a look at the advert, then. What other things can you do?
Mark Well, look, you can go horse-riding – we've both done that. But there's scuba-diving and hang-gliding – we haven't done them.
Louise Oh, it sounds great! Let's write for some details.

Rules

1 **Complete these sentences from exercise 2.**
Mark and Louise _____ ridden a horse.
Louise _____ driven a racing car.

2 **This is the present perfect tense. We use it to talk about experiences in our lives.**

a Compare this with your language.

b The present perfect tense has two parts, the verb *to have* and a past participle. Find these in the sentences above.

c Find examples of these things in **Grammar in use**.
  • negatives
  • short forms

3 How do we make the past participle?

a Some past participles are regular and some are irregular. Find an example of each in the conversation.

b How do we make regular past participles?

c What are the past participles of these verbs? Use the list of irregular verbs on p127 to help you.

watch	go	break	see
live	play	have	be
meet	wear	climb	write

4 How do we make questions in the present perfect tense?

a Complete the questions with these words.

you	has	have	she

1 A _____ _____ ever flown in a helicopter, Louise?
  B No, I _____ .

2 A _____ _____ ever driven a racing car?
  B Yes, she _____ .

b Complete the short answers.

➤ Check the rules for the present perfect tense in **Grammar Reference 14.1**.

Practice

1 Complete the sentences. Put the verbs in brackets into the present perfect tense.

1 Louise _____ (drive) a racing car.
2 Mark _____ (fly) in a helicopter.
3 Maxine _____ (ride) a horse.
4 Mr and Mrs Allison _____ (meet) the US President.
5 Lots of people _____ (see) UFOs.
6 Kelly and Sam _____ (spend) a weekend at a health farm.
7 Todd _____ (play) golf with Tiger Woods.
8 Ryan _____ (appear) on TV.
9 The Wests _____ (win) the lottery twice.
10 Mr and Mrs Taylor _____ (stay) at the most expensive hotel in the world.

2 Look at the pictures and the information.

a Write down what you have / haven't done.

EXAMPLE
I've climbed a mountain

1 climb a mountain   2 break a bone   3 be in a play

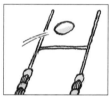  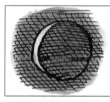

4 win a competition   5 wear a kilt   6 meet a famous person

7 play rugby   8 see an eclipse   9 watch American football

b Make a question about each experience.

EXAMPLE
climb a mountain   *Have you ever climbed a mountain?*

c Think of two more experiences to ask about.

EXAMPLES
Have you ever worked in a shop?
Have you ever had a dog?

d Find a partner. Ask your questions.

EXAMPLE
A *Have you ever climbed a mountain?*
B *Yes, I have / No, I haven't.*

e Find a new partner. Tell him / her about your first partner.

EXAMPLE
Pierre hasn't climbed a mountain. He's broken a bone.

3 Look at these sentences.
A *Have you ever been to Russia?*
B *Yes, I have. I've been to Moscow and St Petersburg.*

a Work with a partner. Find out if he / she has been to these places.
- China
- another country
- a theme park
- the theatre
- a music festival
- a football match
- an art gallery
- a conference
- your capital city
- a pop concert

b How many people in the class have been to each place?

Vocabulary
The world

1 Complete the crossword. Use a dictionary to help you.

Across

Down

2 Can you think of examples of some of the things in the crossword?

EXAMPLE
mountain – Mont Blanc

3 Match the countries and the continents.

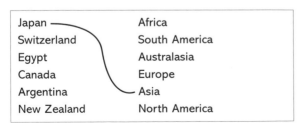

Japan	Africa
Switzerland	South America
Egypt	Australasia
Canada	Europe
Argentina	Asia
New Zealand	North America

Reading and writing
Earthwatch

1 Look at the pictures.
  1 What is happening in each one?
  2 What do you think the text is about?

2 Read the text.
  1 What does Earthwatch do?
  2 Why?
  3 How can you contact Earthwatch?
  4 Which expeditions are shown in the pictures?

3 Which of these things has Will done?
  • studied elephants
  • explored rivers
  • looked for birds
  • dug up dinosaur bones
  • studied the Aztecs
  • planted trees
  • swum in the Pacific Ocean
  • counted whales
  • lived on an island
  • been to Hawaii

◆ EARTHWATCH

HAVE YOU EVER WANTED TO DO SOMETHING DIFFERENT? FIVE YEARS AGO WILL SLADE READ ABOUT AN ORGANIZATION CALLED EARTHWATCH. EARTHWATCH FINDS VOLUNTEERS FOR EXPEDITIONS TO STUDY AND EXPLORE DIFFERENT PARTS OF THE WORLD.

Will decided to join an expedition to study elephants in Africa. 'I wasn't sure about it before I went,' says Will. 'But in fact I really enjoyed every minute of the expedition. We slept in tents and we cooked our own food, but it was great to see the elephants and all the other animals there.'

4 Each paragraph has a sentence missing.

a Read the text again and write the number of each sentence in the correct place.

1 Volunteers have explored the forests and rivers of south-east Asia.
2 Will has now been on three more expeditions.
3 And have you ever wanted to learn more about our planet?
4 I've done so many exciting things, too.
5 It wasn't comfortable.
6 Sometimes we didn't find any, but most days we were lucky.

b Compare your ideas with a partner.

5 What do you think?

1 Is Earthwatch's work important?
2 What kind of expeditions would you like to go on?
3 What would or wouldn't you like about an expedition?

6 Imagine you have been on three expeditions. Write a paragraph.

- Where have you been?
- What did you do on each expedition?
- How do you feel about your experiences?

Language focus: Present perfect and past simple

a Look at these two extracts from the text. What tense is used in each?

Will has now been on three more expeditions. He has counted birds in the rain forests of South America. He has planted trees in Europe and he has studied whales in the Pacific Ocean.

'On my last expedition I was in Hawaii. We got up at 6 a.m. every morning and had our breakfast. Then we went out in the boats and we looked for whales.'

b Which extract is talking about
- Will's experiences up to now?
- a particular experience in the past?

c Complete the rule.

> We use the _____ tense to talk about experiences up to now. We use the _____ tense to talk about a particular experience in the past.

➤ Check your ideas in **Grammar Reference 14.2**.

d Write down five things that you have done. Then write when you did each one.

EXAMPLE
I've flown in a plane.   I flew to Rome two years ago.

He has counted birds in the rain forests of South America. He has planted trees in Europe and he has studied whales in the Pacific Ocean.

'On my last expedition I was in Hawaii. We were on a small island. We got up at 6 a.m. every morning and had our breakfast. Then we went out in the boats and we looked for whales. We spent most of the day in a boat. We photographed the whales, counted them, and we recorded their songs. Whales sing to each other, you know. In the evenings we put all the data into the computer. It was hard work, but we had a lot of fun, and I learnt a lot, too.'

Earthwatch has found volunteers for hundreds of expeditions. They're all ordinary people – male and female, young and old, teachers, students, office workers, engineers. They've dug up dinosaur bones in North America and they've studied ancient civilizations in Central America and Australasia.

Here's Will again. 'I've enjoyed all the expeditions, and I've seen some fantastic places. How many people have slept on a beach, climbed a mountain, or seen a whale? This world is such a beautiful place, but it's disappearing fast. We have to learn more about it if we're going to save it.'

INTERESTED?
Contact Earthwatch:

57 Woodstock Road,
Oxford OX2 6HJ,
United Kingdom

TELEPHONE 44 (0)1865 311600
HOMEPAGE www.earthwatch.org
E-MAIL info@uk.earthwatch.org

Listening and speaking
Lucky Break

1 **Look quickly at the text and the picture.**
  1 Who is the woman?
  2 What is she watching on the TV?

Lucky Break

A few weeks ago Mandy Poole wrote to Sunshine TV. She wanted to be on their breakfast time quiz show, called *Lucky Break*. Mandy loves the show and she watches it every day. She's watching the show now, while she's having her breakfast. She's going to be very surprised soon, because the show's presenter, Russell Dean, has chosen her name and he's going to call her up.

2 Read the text and join the two parts of the sentences.

Mandy loves	the programme every day.
She watches	be very happy.
She wrote	be on the show.
She wanted to	name is Russell Dean.
She's having	*Lucky Break*.
The presenter's	to the TV company.
He's going to	her breakfast at the moment.
Mandy's going to	call her up.

3 📼 *14.2* **Listen to part one and answer the questions.**

1 Where does Mandy live?
2 What does she do?
3 What is her husband's name?
4 What is he doing at the moment?
5 What is the prize?
6 What does Mandy have to do to win the prize?

4 Look at these questions.

1 Is China larger than Russia or smaller than Russia?
2 What are the most dangerous animals in the world?
   ☐ sharks
   ☐ rats
   ☐ snakes
3 Where is the tallest tree in the world?
   ☐ Australia
   ☐ Scotland
   ☐ California
4 Where is the hottest place in the world?
   ☐ the United States
   ☐ India
   ☐ Africa

a What do you think the answers are?
b Do you think Mandy wins?
c 📼 *14.2* Listen to part two and check your ideas.

5 Work in groups of four. Make your own *Lucky Break* quiz show.

a Write down
   • some things for the presenter to ask the contestant about him / herself.
   • a prize for the competition.
   • four quiz questions.
b Choose two people in the group to roleplay the show.
c Change roles and make a new show.

Pronunciation Revision

1 Find the odd one out

a Circle the words with a different vowel sound.

1	wash	watch	catch
2	back	glass	after
3	take	have	plane
4	do	go	so
5	sorry	worry	hurry
6	two	love	move
7	push	pull	but
8	wear	their	ear
9	eye	they	why
10	thin	prize	find

b 📼 *14.3* Listen, check, and repeat.

2 *-es* and *-ed* endings

a How many syllables does each word have?

needed ☐	glasses ☐	lived ☐
takes ☐	goes ☐	used ☐
catches ☐	pages ☐	wanted ☐
walked ☐	practises ☐	danced ☐
loves ☐	dances ☐	badges ☐
stayed ☐	washes ☐	decided ☐
washed ☐	watches ☐	watched ☐

b 📼 *14.4* Listen, check, and repeat.

3 Stress and intonation

a Look at these sentences. Draw the intonation curves.

1 Was the exam <u>difficult</u>?

2 I had a <u>headache</u> <u>yesterday</u>.

3 Why have we got a <u>problem</u>?

4 Are you an <u>engineer</u>?

5 What day is it <u>tomorrow</u>?

6 We <u>arrived</u> in <u>November</u>.

b Look at the underlined words.
   1 Mark (●) the stressed syllable in each word.
   2 Circle the syllables that have the /ə/ sound.

c 📼 *14.5* Listen, check, and repeat.

Extension Units 13 and 14

Language check

going to

1 **Some people have decided to join Earthwatch expeditions. Put in the correct form of *going to*.**
1 I _____ study the ancient civilizations of Mexico.
2 Hans _____ count whales in the Indian Ocean.
3 We _____ join an expedition to the forests of Poland.
4 Mona and José _____ plant trees in Madagascar.
5 Selin _____ look for dinosaur bones.

Present perfect

2 **Complete the sentences. Use the verbs in the box.**

| see   climb   travel   write   swim |

1 Jonathan and Gwen _____ round the world on a motorbike.
2 Felicity _____ across the English Channel.
3 Zach and Duncan _____ the four highest mountains in the world.
4 Suzanne and Angela _____ an alien.
5 Miyako _____ fifty books for children.

Tense revision

3 **Complete the sentences with the correct tense of the verbs in brackets.**
1 Next week we _____ (look for) a new car. We _____ (buy) a sports car. It _____ (be) great to drive.
2 At the moment we _____ (sit) in a café. We _____ (wait) for the museum to open, so I _____ (write) some postcards.
3 Last year we _____ (go) to Greece for our holidays. We _____ (stay) on a small island. We _____ (have) a great time. We _____ (take) lots of photographs.
4 In my life I _____ (visit) lots of different places. I _____ (be) to every continent. And I _____ (fly) round the world twice, too.

Questions

4 **Write the words in the correct order to make questions.**
1 do are ? what going you to
2 to they ? been have Spain
3 did when leave Peter ? university
4 out ? you to do go want
5 phoned ? anyone this has morning
6 going to Lulu ? is us join
7 raining it ? is today
8 driving Mrs does ? Reynolds like
9 waiting we why ? are
10 shall this where evening go we ?

Short answers

5 **Complete the short answers.**
1 A Are you going to the beach?
   B Yes, I _____ .
2 A Have you seen my glasses?
   B No, I _____ .
3 A Is Lucy going to have a party?
   B No, _____ .
4 A Has Stefan written the letter yet?
   B Yes, _____ .
5 A Are City going to win?
   B No, they _____ .

Negatives

6 **Make these sentences negative.**
1 It's going to be cold tomorrow.
2 I've been on holiday.
3 Mr Payne was away yesterday.
4 Katya has lived in a foreign country.
5 We liked the concert.
6 We're leaving.
7 I'm going to give her a ring.
8 Sam likes his job.
9 I need a new jacket.
10 They're going to buy a house.

Conversations

7 **Complete the conversations.**
1 A _____ I help you?
   B Yes. Have you _____ these shorts in a medium _____ , please?
   A Yes, _____ you are.
   B Can I try _____ on?
   A Yes, of _____ . The changing rooms are _____ there.
   Later
   A How _____ they?
   B _____ fine. I'll _____ them.
   A _____ else?
   B No, _____ you.

2 A _____ you like to go out tonight?
   B Oh yes. That would _____ nice. Where _____ we go?
   A _____ go to a club.
   B Good _____ . What _____ shall we go?
   A Oh, about half _____ nine, I think.
   B OK. Shall _____ phone for a taxi?
   A Yes. _____ you know the number?
   B Yes, I _____ .

3 A Hello. I've got _____
appointment _____ Mr Johnson.
B Mr Johnson's _____ room 45.
That's on the fourth _____ . The
_____ are over there.
A Thank you.

Later

A Hello. My _____ Ellen Peters.
B Oh, _____ morning, Ms Peters.
Please _____ a seat. _____ you
like a cup _____ coffee?
A Yes, _____ .
B _____ you want milk _____
sugar?
A Just milk, _____ .
B Here _____ are.
A Thank you.

**8 Make a new conversation for each
of these expressions.**
1 Well, you should go to the doctor's.
2 It opens at 10.30.
3 They're 60p each.
4 Pleased to meet you.

Vocabulary

**9 Look at the Wordlist for Units 13
and 14.**

Write definitions for ten words.

EXAMPLES

millionaire *It's a person with a lot
of money.*

eclipse *It's when the sun goes
behind the moon.*

Extra!
Invent a character

**1 Work with a partner. You are writers for a TV soap opera.
(You can choose a real programme or invent a new one.)**

a You have to invent a new character for the show. Try to think of
an interesting character and give as much information as possible.
Think about these things.

- man / woman
  age
  birthday
- What / look like?
  clothes
- Where / live?
- What / do?
- parents / brothers and sisters
  wife / husband / children
- Where / born?

- Which school / go to?
  like / school?
- What / do after school?
- likes / dislikes
- first appearance
  What / do?
  What / wear?
- future programmes
  What / do?
  What / happen / to him / her?

b Write down the information.

**2 You are going to interview another pair of students about
their new character.**

a Look at the things above. What questions will you ask to get the
information? What tenses will you use?

b Ask about their character.

Grammar Reference

1.1 *a / an*

A / An is the indefinite article.
We use *a* before a consonant.
We use *an* before a vowel.

a man   *an apple*
a girl   *an umbrella*

1.2 The alphabet

This is the English alphabet:

A B C D E F G H I J K L M N O P Q R S T U V W X Y Z

1.3 Plurals

a To make most plurals we add *-s* to the noun.

a cat   *two cats*   one boy   *three boys*

b With words that end in *-ch, -ss, -sh, -x,* or *-o,* we add *-es.*

a watch   *two watches*
a dress   *three dresses*
a brush   *four brushes*
a box   *six boxes*
a tomato   *two tomatoes*

c When the plural ends in *-ches, -sses, -shes, -xes, -ses,* or *-ges,* we pronounce the *-es* ending /ɪz/.

boxes /ˈbɒksɪz/   *oranges* /ˈɒrɪndʒɪz/

d Some plurals are irregular.

a man   *ten men*
a woman   *two women*
a child   *five children*
a person   *four people*

1.4 Adjectives

a We put the adjective in front of the noun.

	adjective	**noun**
a	*new*	*car*
two	*green*	*apples*
	old	*people*

b Adjectives do not change in the plural.

a big house
two big houses

c We use *an* in front of an adjective that begins with a vowel.

an old man   *an orange car*

2.1 The verb *to be*

Positive

I	'm (am)	from Italy.
He She It	's (is)	20.
We You They	're (are)	here.

Negative

I	'm not (am not)	from Italy.
He She It	isn't (is not)	20.
We You They	aren't (are not)	here.

Questions

Am	I	from Italy?
Is	he she it	20?
Are	we you they	here?

Short answers

Yes,	I	am.
	he she it	is.
	we you they	are.

No,	I	'm not. (am not.)
	he she it	isn't. (is not.)
	we you they	aren't. (are not.)

2.2 Imperatives

a For positive commands and requests we use the infinitive of the verb.

Sit down.
Close the door, please.
Come here.

b For negative commands and requests we use *Don't* + the infinitive.

Don't open the door.
Don't look at the photograph.
Don't stand up.

2.3 *a / an* + job

We use *a / an* when we talk about someone's job.

She is a dentist.   NOT ~~She's dentist.~~
I'm an architect.   NOT ~~I'm architect.~~

2.4 Personal pronouns and adjectives

subject pronouns	object pronouns	possessive adjectives
I	me	my
he	him	his
she	her	her
it	it	its
we	us	our
you	you	your
they	them	their

The possessive adjective agrees with the possessor, not the thing that is possessed. We use *his* for men and boys. We use *her* for women and girls.

There's John *with* his *girlfriend.*

And that's Maria *with* her *boyfriend.*

3.1 *have got / has got*

Positive

I We You They	've (have)	got	a mobile phone.
			two brothers.
He She It	's (has)		dark hair.

Note: After words ending in /s/, /z/, /tʃ/, /ʃ/, and /dʒ/ we do not normally use the short form of *has*. We use the full form. In speech this is reduced to /(h)əz/.

Negative

I We You They	haven't (have not)	got	a mobile phone.
			two brothers.
He She It	hasn't (has not)		dark hair.

Questions

Have	I we you they	got	a mobile phone?
			two brothers?
Has	he she it		dark hair?

Short answers

Yes,	I we you they	have.
	he she it	has.

No,	I we you they	haven't. (have not.)
	he she it	hasn't. (has not.)

3.2 Possessive *'s*

To show possession we put *'s* at the end of a name or noun.
Martin's book.
My boyfriend's car.

If the possessor is plural, we put the apostrophe (') after the plural -*s*.
My parents' house.
The boys' names.

3.3 *this, that, these, those*

We use *this / that* with singular nouns and *these / those* with plural nouns.
this woman   these women
that watch   those watches

We use *this / these* for things or people that are near.
We use *that / those* for things or people that are further away.

4.1 *can*

Form

Positive + negative

I He She We You They	can	play the piano.
		swim.
	can't (cannot)	speak Spanish.

Questions

Can	I he she we you they	play the piano?
		swim?
		speak Spanish?

Short answers

Yes,	I he she we you they	can.

No,	I he she we you they	can't. (cannot)

Use

We use *can* to express ability and permission.
ability   *I can't swim.*
permission *You can't swim here.*

4.2 *to play*

We can use the verb *play* with a sport or a musical instrument.
With a sport there is no article.
With a musical instrument there is an article.
I can play basketball.
I can play the violin.

4.3 *have to / has to*

Form

I We You They	have to	go. work tomorrow.
He She It	has to	meet the director.

Use

We use *have to / has to* to show obligation.
I have to go to a conference.
He has to work on Saturdays.

5.1 The present simple tense (1)

Form

Positive

I We You They	like skiing. speak Polish.

Negative

I We You They	don't (do not)	like skiing. speak Polish.

Questions

Do	I we you they	like skiing? speak Polish?

Short answers

Yes,	I we you they	do.	No,	I we you they	don't. (do not.)

Use

We use the present simple tense to describe
- regular events or permanent states.
  I get up at seven o'clock (every day).
  We usually go to the pub in the evening.
  They live in Glasgow.
- general truths.
  Teenagers like hamburgers.
  They speak Spanish in Argentina.

5.2 *like + -ing*

When we use a verb after *like*, we usually use the *-ing* form of the verb.
I like swimming.
Do you like driving?
We prefer playing rugby to watching it.

➤ For the spelling rules of *-ing* forms, see section 11.1.

5.3 Countable and uncountable nouns

a Some nouns are countable. They have a singular and a plural form.
I've got a sandwich.
Here are some sandwiches for you.

I want an apple.
Have you got any apples?

b Some nouns are uncountable. They have no plural form. They use *some* or *any* (see section 5.4).
I need some bread.
I've got some fish for you.
Have you got any coffee?

These things are usually uncountable:
- drinks: *tea, beer, wine, water, coffee, milk*
- food which you only eat part of: *fish, bread, cheese, ham, meat*
- things which you only use part of: *toothpaste, soap, shampoo*
- materials: *paper, wood, wool, plastic*
- some general words: *information, music, money*

Note: Most drinks can be countable or uncountable. They are countable when we can put *cup of* or *glass of* in front of the word.

I'd like a (cup of) coffee, please.	countable
We haven't got any coffee.	uncountable
I'll have a (glass of) red wine, please.	countable
How much wine have we got?	uncountable

c We use *How many ... ?* with countable nouns and *How much ... ?* with uncountable nouns.
How many eggs do we need?
How much cheese have we got?

5.4 *some / any*

Some and *any* are the indefinite articles for plural nouns and uncountable nouns.

We use *some* with positive statements.
We use *any* with negative statements and questions.

We need some new mugs.
We haven't got any apples.
Have you got any pens?

We need some tea.
We haven't got any cheese.
Have you got any water?

6.1 The present simple tense (2)

Positive

I We You They	live work	in Manchester.
He She It	lives works	here.

Spelling
General rule: In the third person singular we add *-s* to the infinitive.

Exceptions: When the verb ends in *-ss*, *-sh*, *-ch*, or *-o*, we add *-es*.

miss	*misses*
wash	*washes*
catch	*catches*
go	*goes*

When the verb ends in consonant + *y,* we change the *-y* to *-ies.*

| hurry | *hurries* |

Pronunciation
After a vowel sound or a voiced consonant we pronounce the final *-s* /z/.

goes /gəʊz/   *comes* /kʌmz/

After a voiceless consonant (/t/, /p/, /k/), we pronounce the final *-s* /s/.

cuts   /kʌts/
stops   /stɒps/
looks   /lʊks/

When the verb ends in *-ges*, *-ches*, *-sses*, *-ses*, or *-shes*, we pronounce *-es* /ɪz/.

changes /ˈtʃeɪndʒɪz/
watches /ˈwɒtʃɪz/
passes /ˈpɑːsɪz/
practises /ˈpræktɪsɪz/
pushes /ˈpʊʃɪz/

Negative

I We You They	don't (do not)	live	in Manchester.
He She It	doesn't (does not)	work	here.

Questions

Do	I we you they	live	in Manchester?
Does	he she it	work	here?

Short answers

Yes,	I we you they	do.
	he she it	does.

No,	I we you they	don't. (do not.)
	he she it	doesn't. (does not.)

Note: In negatives and questions we use the infinitive of the verb.

He doesn't like coffee.   NOT ~~He doesn't likes coffee.~~
Does she play the piano? NOT ~~Does she plays the piano?~~

6.2 Adverbs of frequency
Adverbs of frequency show how often something happens.

never	sometimes	often	usually / normally	always
0				100

We put the adverb of frequency
- in front of a normal verb.
  We often go to a restaurant.
- between an auxiliary verb and the main verb.
  They don't usually have lunch at 12.00.
- after the verb *to be.*
  He's always here at this time.

7.1 *there is / there are*
We use *there is* with singular nouns and *there are* with plural nouns. There is no short form of *there are.*

Positive

There	's (is)	a pen a computer	on the desk.
	are	five pens two computers	

Negative

There	isn't (is not)	a pen a computer	on the desk.
	aren't (are not)	five pens two computers	

Questions

Is	there	a pen a computer	on the desk?
Are		any pens any computers	

Short answers

Yes, there	is. are.

No, there	isn't. (is not.) aren't. (are not.)

7.2 *quite*
We normally put *quite* in front of an adjective.
My family is quite big.
If there is an article, we put *quite* in front of the article.
I've got quite a big family.

8.1 The past simple tense: *was / were*
Positive

I He She It	was	at home	last week.
We You They	were	on holiday	yesterday.

Negative

I He She It	wasn't (was not)	at home	last week.
We You They	weren't (were not)	on holiday	yesterday.

Questions

Was	I he she it	at home	last week?
Were	we you they	on holiday	yesterday?

Short answers

Yes,	I he she it	was.
	we you they	were.

No,	I he she it	wasn't. (was not.)
	we you they	weren't. (were not.)

9.1 The past simple tense: regular verbs

Form

Positive

I He She It We You They	stayed at home watched TV	yesterday. last night.

> **Spelling**
>
> When the verb ends in -e, we add -d.
> live — lived
> practise — practised
>
> When the verb ends in a short vowel and a single consonant, we double the consonant and add -ed.
> stop — stopped
> grab — grabbed
>
> When the verb ends in a consonant + y, we change the -y to -ied.
> carry — carried
> try — tried

> **Pronunciation**
>
> After a vowel sound or a voiced consonant we pronounce the final -d /d/.
> pulled /pʊld/   lived /lɪvd/
>
> After a voiceless consonant (/p/, /k/, /tʃ/, /ʃ/, /s/) we pronounce the final -d /t/.
> stopped /stɒpt/   watched /wɒtʃt/
> looked /lʊkt/   missed /mɪst/
>
> After -t or -d we pronounce the final syllable /ɪd/.
> started /'stɑːtɪd/   needed /'niːdɪd/

Negative

I He She It We You They	didn't (did not)	stay at home watch TV	yesterday. last night.

Questions

Did	I he she it we you they	stay at home watch TV	yesterday? last night?

Short answers

Yes,	I he she it we you they	did.

No,	I he she it we you they	didn't. (did not.)

Note: In negatives and questions we use the infinitive of the verb.
She didn't like the film.   NOT ~~She didn't liked the film.~~
Did you wash up?   NOT ~~Did you washed up?~~

Use

We use the past simple tense to describe
* a completed action in the past.

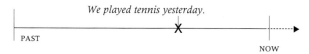
We played tennis yesterday.

* a completed situation in the past.

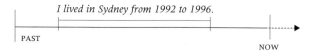
I lived in Sydney from 1992 to 1996.

* a repeated action in the past.

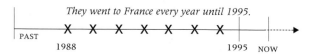
They went to France every year until 1995.

➤ See the present perfect tense (section 14.1).

9.2 *ago*

We use *ago* to say how long before the present something happened. We put *ago* after the time expression.
He arrived two hours ago.
We lived here ten years ago.

10.1 The past simple tense: irregular verbs

Positive

Many common verbs have an irregular past form.

infinitive	past simple
do	*I did it last week.*
see	*We saw him yesterday.*

The irregular form is the same for all persons.
➤ See the list of irregular verbs on p127.

Negatives, questions, short answers

Negatives, questions, and short answers are the same as for regular verbs.
I didn't go to the USA.
I didn't buy a car.

Did you have a good holiday?
Did you see James yesterday?

Yes, we did.
No, I didn't.
➤ See section 9.1.

11.1 The present continuous tense

Form

Positive

I	'm (am)	studying history.
He She It	's (is)	having lunch.
We You They	're (are)	going to work.

Negative

I	'm not (am not)	studying history.
He She It	isn't (is not)	having lunch.
We You They	aren't (are not)	going to work.

Questions

Am	I	studying history?
Is	he she it	having lunch?
Are	we you they	going to work?

Short answers

Yes,	I	am.
	he she it	is.
	we you they	are.

No,	I	'm not. (am not.)
	he she it	isn't. (is not.)
	we you they	aren't. (are not.)

> **Spelling**
>
> **General rule:** We add *-ing* to the infinitive.
> cook *cooking*
>
> **Exceptions:** For verbs that end in *-e*, we remove the *-e* and add *-ing*.
> write *writing*   practise *practising*
>
> For verbs with a short vowel and only one consonant, we double the consonant and add *-ing*.
> run *running*   sit *sitting*

Use

We use the present continuous tense to
- say what is happening at the moment.
  We're watching TV at the moment.
  'Where's Jane?' 'She's having a bath.'

- describe a temporary state or limited period of time.
  I'm studying at university.
  She's playing tennis this week.

11.2 Present simple and present continuous

The present simple describes a regular event or a permanent state.
regular event   *We usually have lunch at 2.00.*
permanent state   *I work in an office.*

The present continuous describes what is happening at the moment, or a temporary state.
at the moment   *Margaret isn't here – she's doing the shopping.*
temporary state   *This week we're having lunch at 1.00.*

Look at these sentences. In each pair one is right (✓) and one is wrong (✗).
1 I go to the cinema every week. ✓
   I'm going to the cinema every week. ✗
2 She gets up at 6.00 every day. ✓
   She's getting up at 6.00 every day. ✗
3 A Where's John?
   B He's playing tennis. ✓
   A Where's John?
   B He plays tennis. ✗
4 I'm staying with my parents this week. ✓
   I stay with my parents this week. ✗
5 Vegetarians don't eat meat. ✓
   Vegetarians aren't eating meat. ✗
6 A What do you do?
   B I'm a teacher. ✓
   A What do you do?
   B I watch a film. ✗

➤ Look at the **Use** sections for the present simple (section 5.1) and the present continuous and check the rules.

11.3 Clothes

The names of some clothes are always plural.

jeans   trousers   shorts

These words take plural articles and plural verbs.

A *How much is this shirt?*
B *It's £25.*
A *How much are these trousers?*
B *They're £50.*

12.1 Comparatives and superlatives

	adjective	comparative	superlative
one syllable	young cold	younger colder	the youngest the coldest
one syllable – ending in -e	nice late	nicer later	the nicest the latest
one syllable – short vowel + one consonant	wet thin big	wetter thinner bigger	the wettest the thinnest the biggest
two syllables – consonant + y	heavy sunny	heavier sunnier	the heaviest the sunniest
two or more syllables	attractive interesting	more attractive more interesting	the most attractive the most interesting
irregular	good bad far	better worse further	the best the worst the furthest

12.2 *should / shouldn't*

Form

Positive + negative

I He She We You They	should	leave now.
	shouldn't (should not)	have a rest.

Questions

Should	I he she we you they	make the bed? tell him?

Short answers

Yes,	I he she	should.
No,	we you they	shouldn't. (should not.)

Use

We use *should / shouldn't* to give advice.
You should stay at home.
You shouldn't go to work.

13.1 *going to*

Form

Positive

I	'm (am)		
He She It	's (is)	going to	watch TV. have a drink. buy a new car.
We You They	're (are)		

Negative

I	'm not (am not)		
He She It	isn't (is not)	going to	watch TV. have a drink. buy a new car.
We You They	aren't (are not)		

Questions

Am	I		
Is	he she it	going to	watch TV? have a drink? buy a new car?
Are	we you they		

Short answers

Yes,	I	am.
	he she it	is.
	we you they	are.

No,	I	'm not. (am not.)
	he she it	isn't. (is not.)
	we you they	aren't. (are not.)

Use

We use *going to* to talk about plans and intentions.
I'm going to paint the kitchen this weekend.
We're going to move to Edinburgh next year.

13.2 Phrasal verbs

Some verbs in English have two parts. We call these phrasal verbs. With some phrasal verbs the meaning is clear from the meanings of the two parts.

stand up
sit down

With some phrasal verbs we can't work out the meaning from the individual parts.

break down
sort out

With a lot of phrasal verbs we can put the second part after the object.

He picked up the pen.
He picked the pen up.

Put down your book.
Put your book down.

14.1 The present perfect tense

Form

Positive

| I
We
You
They | 've
(have) | ridden a horse.

slept on a beach. |
| He
She
It | 's
(has) | lived in Africa. |

Note: After words ending in /s/, /z/, /tʃ/, /ʃ/, and /dʒ/ we do not normally use the short form of *has*. We use the full form. In speech this is reduced to /(h)əz/.

Negative

| I
We
You
They | haven't
(have not) | ridden a horse.

slept on a beach. |
| He
She
It | hasn't
(has not) | lived in Africa. |

Questions

| Have | I
we
you
they | ridden a horse?

slept on a beach? |
| Has | he
she
it | lived in Africa? |

Short answers

| Yes, | I
we
you
they | have. | No, | I
we
you
they | haven't.
(have not.) |
| | he
she
it | has. | | he
she
it | hasn't.
(has not.) |

We make the present perfect tense with *have / has* and the past participle of the verb.
To form regular past participles, we add *-ed* to the infinitive.

wait *waited*
stay *stayed*

This is the same as the regular past tense.
➤ See section 9.1 for spelling and pronunciation rules.

A lot of common verbs have an irregular past participle.

go *gone*
see *seen*
swim *swum*
write *written*

➤ See the list of irregular verbs on p127.

Use

We use the present perfect to talk about experiences in our life, when we don't say when the experience happened.

I've been to Egypt.
Have you ever seen a UFO?

been

In the present perfect tense we use *been* instead of *gone* when we are talking about our experiences.

A *Have you ever been to Mexico?*
B *Yes, I have.*
A *Oh, when did you go?*

A *We went hang-gliding yesterday.*
B *Oh, really? I've never been hang gliding*

14.2 Present perfect and past simple

We use the present perfect to talk about experiences in our life. We use the past simple when we say when something happened.

I've been to Egypt three times. Last year I went to Cairo.

Note: When there is a past time reference (*in 1987, two days ago, yesterday*), we use the past simple tense, not the present perfect. Look at these sentences.

1 I went to the United States in 1998. ✓
   I've been to the United States in 1998. ✗
2 I broke my leg last year. ✓
   I've broken my leg last year. ✗

Functional Language

Useful expressions

How do you spell | your name?
| that?
| *umbrella*?

A What does _____ mean?   **B** It means _____ .
                                B I don't know.

I'm sorry, I don't understand.

How do you pronounce | your name?
                     | this word?

A Can you repeat that, please?
B Yes, of course.

What's this called in English?
How do you say _____ in English?

Meeting people

A Hi. How are you?
B Fine, thanks. And you?
A Oh, not bad.

A Pleased to meet you.
B Nice to meet you, too.

A What's your name?
B My name's _____ .
B I'm _____ .

A What's your address?
B It's _____ .
A What's your (tele)phone number?
B It's _____ .

A Where are you from?
B I'm from _____ .

A How do you do?
B How do you do?

A What do you do?
B I'm a student / bank clerk / doctor. What about you?

Excuse me. Are you _____ ?
Goodbye / Bye.

Shopping

Customer

Have you got any | mugs?
                 | oranges?

How much is this | pen?
                 | CD player?

How much are | these watches?
             | those posters?

Can I have | this dictionary, please?
           | these postcards, please?

I'll have | these two, please.
          | this one, please.

Can I pay by credit card?
Do you take credit cards?

Assistant

Can I help you?
It's £10.50.
They're £7.25 (each).
Anything else?
Do you want anything else?
That's £52.75 (altogether).
Here you are.
That's £1.25 change.
Could you sign here, please?

Buying clothes

How much | is this T-shirt?
         | are these jeans?

Have you got it / them in | a size 32?
                          | a size 10?
                          | small / medium / large?

Can I try it / them on?
The changing rooms are over there.
How is it / are they?
It's / They're fine, thanks.
I'll take it / them.

Telling the time

eight o'clock

five past three

ten past nine

quarter past two

twenty past seven

twenty-five past twelve

half past five

twenty-five to six

twenty to ten

quarter to one

ten to eleven

five to four

We can also give times in digital form.
4.30   *four thirty*
12.42   *twelve forty-two*
17.06   *seventeen oh six*

Arranging a meeting

Can you play tennis	on Sunday?
	tomorrow?
	this afternoon?

Can we meet	at 2.00?
	on Monday?
	at the weekend?

A Is Thursday OK for you?
B No, that's no good, I'm afraid.
B No, I'm sorry. Thursday's no good for me.

A What about Friday?
B Yes, that's OK.
B Yes, that's fine.
B Yes, Friday's all right for me.

See you on Friday.

I'm sorry. I can't	come to the cinema this evening.
I'm afraid I can't	play football tomorrow.
	make it.

Offering and accepting

A Would you like	a drink?
	a cup of coffee?
	something to eat?

B Yes, please.
B No, thanks, I'm fine.

| **A** Do you want | ice and lemon? |
| | milk and sugar? |

B Yes, please.
B Just milk, please.
B No, thanks.

A What would you like (to drink)?
B I'll have a glass of wine, please.
B A cup of tea, please.

Asking where something is

| Is there | a post office | here? |
| | a fax machine | |

| Excuse me. Where's | the toilet? |
| | the restaurant? |

| Where can I find | Mrs Wilson? |
| | the photocopier? |

| Where can I buy some | stamps? |
| | postcards? |

| Is the restaurant | on the third floor? |
| | on the ground floor? |

Saying where something is

It's on the	first
	second	floor.
	third

She's in room 2354.

It's the	first	door	on the left.
	second	building	on the right.
	third		

The lifts are behind you.
Take the lift up to the sixth floor.

| It's on the | left. |
| | right. |

113

Dates

We write dates like this:
25 April (or *April 25*)
3 December (or *December 3*)

We say dates like this:
the twenty-fifth of April (or *April the twenty-fifth*)
the third of December (or *December the third*)

Travel arrangements

Customer

| I'd like a hotel near | the centre. |
| | the airport. |

| We'd like to go | by train. |
| | by boat. |

| I'd like to book | a trip to Italy. |
| | a flight to New York. |

| How long is | the flight? |
| | the journey? |

| We want to spend | about two weeks there. |
| | three days there. |

Travel agent

| When do you want to | travel? |
| | go? |

Do you need accommodation?
How many people is it for?
Is it for two people?
How would you like to travel?
How long do you want to go for?

Talking about problems / illness

Asking about problems

What's the matter?
What's wrong?
Are you all right?
What's up?

Describing the problem

I'm	cold.
	hot.
	hungry.
	thirsty.
	tired.

I've got	a headache.
	toothache.
	stomach ache.
	a cold.
	a cough.
	a sore throat.

My	eye	hurts.
	ear	
	back	
	arm	

I don't feel well.

Making suggestions

| Let's | go to the cinema. |
| | have a pizza. |

Shall we	go out?
Why don't we	eat out tonight?
Would you like to	go on holiday?

Agreeing

That would be nice.
Good idea.
Yes, OK.
Great idea!
That would be great.

Disagreeing and giving alternatives

I'm afraid I can't. I have to ...
Sorry, I can't. I have to ...
No, I don't really like ...

I'm afraid I'm a bit busy	at the moment.
	this evening.
	this weekend.

I don't really feel like it.

How about	tomorrow?
What about	next weekend?
	a Chinese meal?

Wordlist

Unit 1
Hello
capital /'kæpɪtl/
from /frɒm, frəm/
name /neɪm/
where /weə(r)/

Argentina /ˌɑːʤən'tiːnə/
Brazil /brə'zɪl/
France /frɑːns/
Hungary /'hʌŋgəri/
Italy /'ɪtəli/
Japan /ʤə'pæn/
Poland /'pəʊlənd/
Spain /speɪn/
Switzerland /'swɪtsələnd/
Turkey /'tɜːki/
the UK /ðə ˌjuː 'keɪ/
the USA /ðə ˌjuː es 'eɪ/

Numbers
1 one /wʌn/
2 two /tuː/
3 three /θriː/
4 four /fɔː(r)/
5 five /faɪv/
6 six /sɪks/
7 seven /'sevn/
8 eight /eɪt/
9 nine /naɪn/
10 ten /ten/
11 eleven /ɪ'levn/
12 twelve /twelv/
13 thirteen /ˌθɜː'tiːn/
14 fourteen /ˌfɔː'tiːn/
15 fifteen /ˌfɪf'tiːn/
16 sixteen /ˌsɪks'tiːn/
17 seventeen /ˌsevn'tiːn/
18 eighteen /ˌeɪ'tiːn/
19 nineteen /ˌnaɪn'tiːn/
20 twenty /'twenti/
21 twenty-one
   /ˌtwenti 'wʌn/
22 twenty-two
   /ˌtwenti 'tuː/
30 thirty /'θɜːti/
40 forty /'fɔːti/
50 fifty /'fɪfti/
60 sixty /'sɪksti/
70 seventy /'sevnti/
80 eighty /'eɪti/
90 ninety /'naɪnti/
100 a / one hundred
   /ə, ˌwʌn 'hʌndrəd/

Classroom language
alphabet /'ælfəbet/
apple /'æpl/
bag /bæg/
book /bʊk/
boy /bɔɪ/
desk /desk/
dictionary /'dɪkʃənri/
girl /gɜːl/
goodbye /gʊd'baɪ/
man /mæn/
to mean /miːn/
to meet /miːt/
notebook /'nəʊtbʊk/

orange /'ɒrɪnʤ/
pen /pen/
please /pliːz/
to pronounce /prə'naʊns/
to repeat /rɪ'piːt/
to say /seɪ/
sorry /'sɒri/
to spell /spel/
student /'stjuːdənt/
teacher /'tiːtʃə(r)/
umbrella /ʌm'brelə/
to understand
   /ˌʌndə'stænd/
what /wɒt/
woman /'wʊmən/
word /wɜːd/

Personal information
address /ə'dres/
age /eɪʤ/
number /'nʌmbə(r)/
phone /fəʊn/
telephone /'telɪfəʊn/

Plurals
badge /bæʤ/
box /bɒks/
child /tʃaɪld/
children /'tʃɪldrən/
dress (n) /dres/
men /men/
people /'piːpl/
person /'pɜːsn/
toothbrush /'tuːθbrʌʃ/
watch (n) /wɒtʃ/
women /'wɪmɪn/

Adjectives
bad /bæd/
big /bɪg/
cheap /tʃiːp/
colour /'kʌlə(r)/
expensive /ɪk'spensɪv/
fast /fɑːst/
fat /fæt/
good /gʊd/
heavy /'hevi/
light /laɪt/
new /njuː/
old /əʊld/
short /ʃɔːt/
slim /slɪm/
slow /sləʊ/
small /smɔːl/
tall /tɔːl/
thick /θɪk/
thin /θɪn/
young /jʌŋ/

Colours
black /blæk/
blue /bluː/
brown /braʊn/
green /griːn/
grey /greɪ/
orange /'ɒrɪnʤ/
pink /pɪŋk/
purple /'pɜːpl/
red /red/
white /waɪt/
yellow /'jeləʊ/

In a café
anything else /ˌenɪθɪŋ 'els/
cheeseburger /'tʃiːzbɜːgə(r)/
coffee /'kɒfi/
cola /'kəʊlə/
French fries /ˌfrentʃ 'fraɪz/
hamburger /'hæmbɜːgə(r)/
hot dog /'hɒt ˌdɒg/
large /lɑːʤ/
lemonade /leməˈneɪd/
menu /'menjuː/
orange juice /'ɒrɪnʤ ˌʤuːs/
pence /pens/
pizza /'piːtsə/
pound /paʊnd/
price /praɪs/
tea /tiː/

Unit 2
Grammar
America /ə'merɪkə/
to be /biː, bi/
Canada /'kænədə/
city /'sɪti/
Excuse me. /ɪk'skjuːz ˌmiː/
favourite /'feɪvərɪt/
here /'hɪə(r)/
meeting /'miːtɪŋ/
Mr /'mɪstə(r)/
Mrs /'mɪsɪz/
Ms /mz/
on holiday /ˌɒn 'hɒlədeɪ/
over there /ˌəʊvə 'ðeə(r)/
partner /'pɑːtnə(r)/
Portugal /'pɔːtʃʊgl/
room /ruːm/

Vocabulary
board /bɔːd/
to close /kləʊz/
to come /kʌm/
exercise /'eksesaɪz/
to go /gəʊ/
to listen /'lɪsn/
to look (at) /lʊk/
to open /'əʊpən/
page /peɪʤ/
to pick up /ˌpɪk 'ʌp/
to put down /ˌpʊt 'daʊn/
to read /riːd/
to say /seɪ/
to sit down /ˌsɪt 'daʊn/
to stand up /ˌstænd 'ʌp/
to turn /tɜːn/
to write /raɪt/

Reading
and /ænd, ənd/
at /æt, ət/
Australia /ɒ'streɪliə/
Belgium /'belʤəm/
boyfriend /'bɔɪfrend/
to do /duː/
garden /'gɑːdn/
girlfriend /'gɜːlfrend/
house /haʊs/
husband /'hʌzbənd/
India /'ɪndiə/
job /ʤɒb/
married /'mærɪd/

parents /'peərənts/
photo /'fəʊtəʊ/
wife /waɪf/
with /wɪð/
(20) years old /ˌjɪəz 'əʊld/

Jobs
architect /'ɑːkɪtekt/
bank clerk /'bæŋk ˌklɑːk/
dentist /'dentɪst/
doctor /'dɒktə(r)/
engineer /enʤɪ'nɪə(r)/
hairdresser /'heədresə(r)/
nurse /nɜːs/
pilot /'paɪlət/
secretary /'sekrətri/
shop assistant
   /'ʃɒp əˌsɪstənt/
waiter /'weɪtə(r)/
waitress /'weɪtrəs/

Listening
about /ə'baʊt/
to feel /fiːl/
fine /faɪn/
friend /frend/
guy /gaɪ/
how /haʊ/
interesting /'ɪntrəstɪŋ/
just a minute /ˌʤʌst ə
   'mɪnɪt/
kid /kɪd/
to meet /miːt/
party /'pɑːti/
thanks /θæŋks/
too /tuː/
who /huː/

Extension
Units 1 and 2
Greece /griːs/
interview (n) /'ɪntəvjuː/
language school /'læŋgwɪʤ
   ˌskuːl/
surname /'sɜːneɪm/

Unit 3
Grammar
brother /'brʌðə(r)/
camera /'kæmərə/
car /kɑː(r)/
CD player /ˌsiː'diː
   ˌpleɪə(r)/
colour /'kʌlə(r)/
computer /kəm'pjuːtə(r)/
dark /dɑːk/
dog /dɒg/
eye /aɪ/
fair /feə(r)/
fax /fæks/
glasses /'glɑːsɪz/
hair /heə(r)/
mobile phone /ˌməʊbaɪl
   'fəʊn/
pet /pet/
sister /'sɪstə(r)/
which /wɪtʃ/

Vocabulary

attractive /ə'træktɪv/
bald /bɔːld/
beard /bɪəd/
blond(e) /blɒnd/
family /'fæməli/
famous /'feɪməs/
good-looking /ˌgʊd 'lʊkɪŋ/
long /lɒŋ/
member /'membə(r)/
middle-aged /ˌmɪdl 'eɪdʒd/
moustache /mə'stɑːʃ/
quite /kwaɪt/
ugly /'ʌgli/
very /'veri/

Reading

baby /'beɪbi/
female /'fiːmeɪl/
identical /aɪ'dentɪkl/
male /meɪl/
older /'əʊldə(r)/
single /'sɪŋgl/
Sweden /'swiːdn/
younger /'jʌŋgə(r)/

Families

aunt /ɑːnt/
cousin /'kʌzn/
daughter /'dɔːtə(r)/
father /'fɑːðə(r)/
grandchildren /'græntʃɪldrən/
granddaughter /'grændɔːtə(r)/
grandfather /'grænfɑːðə(r)/
grandmother /'grænmʌðə(r)/
grandparents /'grænpeərənts/
grandson /'grænsʌn/
mother /'mʌðə(r)/
nephew /'nefjuː/
niece /niːs/
son /sʌn/
twins /twɪnz/
uncle /'ʌŋkl/

Listening

altogether /ˌɔːltə'geðə(r)/
to buy /baɪ/
change (n) /tʃeɪndʒ/
to cost /kɒst/
each /iːtʃ/
How many ...? /'haʊ ˌmeni/
How much ...? /'haʊ ˌmʌtʃ/
key-ring /'kiː rɪŋ/
mug /mʌg/
postcard /'pəʊstkɑːd/
poster /'pəʊstə(r)/
strap /stræp/
T-shirt /'tiː ʃɜːt/
thing /θɪŋ/

Unit 4

Grammar

basketball /'bɑːskɪtbɔːl/
bicycle /'baɪsɪkl/
to cook /kʊk/
to dance /dɑːns/
to drive /draɪv/
drums /drʌmz/

football /'fʊtbɔːl/
foreign /'fɒrən/
free time /ˌfriː 'taɪm/
golf /gɒlf/
guitar /gɪ'tɑː(r)/
to hear /hɪə(r)/
to help /help/
horse /hɔːs/
language /'læŋgwɪdʒ/
musical instrument /ˌmjuːzɪkl 'ɪnstrəmənt/
piano /pi'ænəʊ/
to play /pleɪ/
to ride /raɪd/
rugby /'rʌgbi/
to run /rʌn/
saxophone /'sæksəfəʊn/
to sing /sɪŋ/
to ski /skiː/
to speak /spiːk/
sport /spɔːt/
to swim /swɪm/
tennis /'tenɪs/
to turn up /ˌtɜːn 'ʌp/
violin /vaɪə'lɪn/

Vocabulary

afternoon /ˌɑːftə'nuːn/
appointment /ə'pɔɪntmənt/
conference /'kɒnfərəns/
day /deɪ/
evening /'iːvnɪŋ/
game /geɪm/
midnight /'mɪdnaɪt/
morning /'mɔːnɪŋ/
night /naɪt/
radio /'reɪdiəʊ/
tomorrow /tə'mɒrəʊ/
week /wiːk/
weekday /'wiːkdeɪ/
the weekend /ðə wiː'kend/
What's the time? /ˌwɒts ðə 'taɪm/

Days of the week

Monday /'mʌndeɪ/
Tuesday /'tjuːzdeɪ/
Wednesday /'wenzdeɪ/
Thursday /'θɜːzdeɪ/
Friday /'fraɪdeɪ/
Saturday /'sætədeɪ/
Sunday /'sʌndeɪ/

Reading

to agree /ə'griː/
alcoholic /ˌælkə'hɒlɪk/
also /'ɔːlsəʊ/
because /bɪ'kɒz/
bus /bʌs/
cigarette /ˌsɪgə'ret/
country /'kʌntri/
drink (n) /drɪŋk/
election /ɪ'lekʃn/
to gamble /'gæmbl/
to get a job /ˌget ə 'dʒɒb/
to get married /ˌget 'mærɪd/
home /həʊm/
into /'ɪntuː, 'ɪntə/
to leave /liːv/
lorry /'lɒri/
moped /'məʊped/
motorbike /'məʊtəbaɪk/
part-time /ˌpɑːt 'taɪm/

school /skuːl/
to smoke /sməʊk/
to vote /vəʊt/
until /ʌn'tɪl/
why /waɪ/

Listening

all right /ˌɔːl 'raɪt/
arrangement /ə'reɪndʒmənt/
cinema /'sɪnəmə/
diary /'daɪəri/
to finish /'fɪnɪʃ/
to go shopping /ˌgəʊ 'ʃɒpɪŋ/
to have lunch /ˌhæv 'lʌntʃ/
lunch /lʌntʃ/
to make /meɪk/
manager /'mænɪdʒə(r)/
OK /əʊ'keɪ/
receptionist /rɪ'sepʃənɪst/
report (n) /rɪ'pɔːt/
somewhere /'sʌmweə(r)/
to spend (time) /spend/
to visit /'vɪzɪt/
visitor /'vɪzɪtə(r)/
when /wen/

Extension

Units 3 and 4

heart /hɑːt/
I love you. /ˌaɪ 'lʌv juː/
squash /skwɒʃ/

Unit 5

Grammar

cat /kæt/
Chinese /tʃaɪ'niːz/
to drink /drɪŋk/
food /fuːd/
to learn /lɜːn/
to like /laɪk/
opera /'ɒprə/
pop music /'pɒp ˌmjuːzɪk/
to prefer /prɪ'fɜː(r)/
restaurant /'restrɒnt/
snowboarding /'snəʊbɔːdɪŋ/
That's a pity. /'ðæts ə ˌpɪti/
ticket /'tɪkɪt/
to work /wɜːk/

Vocabulary

bacon /'beɪkən/
banana /bə'nɑːnə/
beer /bɪə(r)/
bread /bred/
cheese /tʃiːz/
to eat /iːt/
egg /eg/
fish /fɪʃ/
fruit /fruːt/
meat /miːt/
milk /mɪlk/
mushroom /'mʌʃruːm/
pasta /'pæstə/
potato /pə'teɪtəʊ/
rice /raɪs/
sandwich /'sænwɪdʒ/
sausage /'sɒsɪdʒ/
tomato /tə'mɑːtəʊ/
vegetable /'vedʒtəbl/
water /'wɔːtə(r)/
wine /waɪn/

Reading

biscuit /'bɪskɪt/
both /bəʊθ/
breakfast /'brekfəst/
cake /keɪk/
a cup of /ə 'kʌp əv/
dessert /dɪ'zɜːt/
dinner /'dɪnə(r)/
farm /fɑːm/
a few /ə 'fjuː/
a glass of /ə 'glɑːs əv/
to go to work /ˌgəʊ tə 'wɜːk/
ham /hæm/
ice cream /ˌaɪs 'kriːm/
Italian /ɪ'tæliən/
meal /miːl/
perhaps /pə'hæps/
pie /paɪ/
a pint of /ə 'paɪnt əv/
pub /pʌb/
pudding /'pʊdɪŋ/
salad /'sæləd/
soup /suːp/
to start /stɑːt/
toast /təʊst/

Listening

ice /aɪs/
lemon /'lemən/
mineral water /'mɪnərəl ˌwɔːtə(r)/
sugar /'ʃʊgə(r)/
to want /wɒnt/

Unit 6

Grammar

bank /bæŋk/
to communicate /kə'mjuːnɪkeɪt/
company /'kʌmpəni/
e-mail /'iː ˌmeɪl/
to enjoy /ɪn'dʒɔɪ/
every day /ˌevri 'deɪ/
to go back (to) /ˌgəʊ 'bæk/
lifestyle /'laɪfstaɪl/
to live /lɪv/
newspaper /'njuːspeɪpə(r)/
really /'riːəli/
train (n) /treɪn/
to travel /'trævl/

Vocabulary

to catch /kætʃ/
to clean /kliːn/
to come home /ˌkʌm 'həʊm/
crossword /'krɒswɜːd/
to get dressed /ˌget 'drest/
to get up /ˌget 'ʌp/
to go to bed /ˌgəʊ tə 'bed/
to have a shower /ˌhæv ə 'ʃaʊə(r)/
teeth /tiːθ/
TV /tiː'viː/
to wake up /ˌweɪk 'ʌp/
to wash up /ˌwɒʃ 'ʌp/
to watch /wɒtʃ/

Reading

after /'ɑːftə(r)/
again /ə'gen/

to arrive /əˈraɪv/
before /bɪˈfɔː(r)/
busy /ˈbɪzi/
cake /keɪk/
chalet /ˈʃæleɪ/
club /klʌb/
to come back /ˌkʌm ˈbæk/
different /ˈdɪfrənt/
early /ˈɜːli/
to go out /ˌgəʊ ˈaʊt/
to go skiing /ˌgəʊ ˈskiːɪŋ/
group /gruːp/
guest /gest/
to have a rest /ˌhæv ə ˈrest/
to look after /ˌlʊk ˈɑːftə(r)/
resort /rɪˈzɔːt/
shop /ʃɒp/
skier /ˈskiːə(r)/
supermarket /ˈsuːpəˌmɑːkɪt/
to take /teɪk/
then /ðen/
to tidy /ˈtaɪdi/
to walk /wɔːk/

Adverbs of frequency
always /ˈɔːlweɪz/
usually /ˈjuːʒʊəli/
normally /ˈnɔːməli/
often /ˈɒfn, ˈɒftən/
sometimes /ˈsʌmtaɪmz/
never /ˈnevə(r)/

Listening
film (n) /fɪlm/
to happen /ˈhæpən/
lesson /ˈlesn/
museum /mjuːˈzɪəm/
normal /ˈnɔːml/
office hours /ˈɒfɪs ˌaʊəz/
plane /pleɪn/
programme /ˈprəʊgræm/
to record /rɪˈkɔːd/
school day /ˈskuːl ˌdeɪ/
to teach /tiːtʃ/
working day /ˈwɜːkɪŋ ˌdeɪ/

Extension
Units 5 and 6
butter /ˈbʌtə(r)/
Chile /ˈtʃɪli/
late /leɪt/
library /ˈlaɪbrəri/
reporter /rɪˈpɔːtə(r)/

Unit 7
Grammar
assistant /əˈsɪstənt/
to attack /əˈtæk/
class /klɑːs/
director /dəˈrektə(r)/
floor /flɔː(r)/
great /greɪt/
hero /ˈhɪərəʊ/
hotel /həʊˈtel/
pencil /ˈpensl/
picture /ˈpɪktʃə(r)/
problem /ˈprɒbləm/
scene /siːn/
steps /steps/
street /striːt/
traffic /ˈtræfɪk/

wall /wɔːl/
what else /ˌwɒt ˈels/
window /ˈwɪndəʊ/

Prepositions of position
behind /bɪˈhaɪnd/
between /bɪˈtwiːn/
in /ɪn/
in front of /ɪn ˈfrʌnt əv/
next to /ˈneks tə/
on /ɒn/
opposite /ˈɒpəzɪt/
under /ˈʌndə(r)/

Vocabulary
armchair /ˈɑːmtʃeə(r)/
bath /bɑːθ/
bookcase /ˈbʊkkeɪs/
chair /tʃeə(r)/
chest of drawers /ˌtʃest əv ˈdrɔːz/
coffee table /ˈkɒfi ˌteɪbl/
cooker /ˈkʊkə(r)/
cupboard /ˈkʌbəd/
curtain /ˈkɜːtən/
fridge /frɪdʒ/
mirror /ˈmɪrə(r)/
shower /ˈʃaʊə(r)/
sink /sɪŋk/
sofa /ˈsəʊfə/
table /ˈteɪbl/
television /ˈtelɪvɪʒn/
wardrobe /ˈwɔːdrəʊb/
washbasin /ˈwɒʃbeɪsn/
washing machine /ˈwɒʃɪŋ məˌʃiːn/

Parts of a house
bathroom /ˈbɑːθruːm/
bedroom /ˈbedruːm/
dining room /ˈdaɪnɪŋ ˌruːm/
garage /ˈgærɑːʒ, ˈgærɪdʒ/
hall /hɔːl/
kitchen /ˈkɪtʃɪn/
living room /ˈlɪvɪŋ ˌruːm/
toilet /ˈtɔɪlət/

Reading
almost /ˈɔːlməʊst/
apart from /əˈpɑːt frəm/
argument /ˈɑːgjʊmənt/
away /əˈweɪ/
back /bæk/
boat /bəʊt/
but /bʌt/
centre /ˈsentə(r)/
convenient /kənˈviːniənt/
downstairs /ˌdaʊnˈsteəz/
everything /ˈevrɪθɪŋ/
farm /fɑːm/
farmhouse /ˈfɑːmhaʊs/
flat (n) /flæt/
friendly /ˈfrendli/
front /frʌnt/
fun (n) /fʌn/
houseboat /ˈhaʊsbəʊt/
in the country /ˌɪn ðə ˈkʌntri/
inside /ˌɪnˈsaɪd/
to keep /kiːp/
mile /maɪl/

to move /muːv/
near /nɪə(r)/
neighbour /ˈneɪbə(r)/
other /ˈʌðə(r)/
outside /ˌaʊtˈsaɪd/
pub /pʌb/
quiet /ˈkwaɪət/
to share /ʃeə(r)/
to sleep /sliːp/
suburb /ˈsʌbɜːb/
the best /ðə ˈbest/
theatre /ˈθɪətə/
town /taʊn/
university /ˌjuːnɪˈvɜːsəti/
upstairs /ʌpˈsteəz/
view /vjuː/
village /ˈvɪlɪdʒ/
wonderful /ˈwʌndəfl/

Listening
building /ˈbɪldɪŋ/
escalator /ˈeskəleɪtə(r)/
to find /faɪnd/
floor /flɔː(r)/
to get off /ˌget ˈɒf/
level /ˈlevl/
lift (n) /lɪft/
on the left /ˌɒn ðə ˈleft/
on the right /ˌɒn ðə ˈraɪt/
post office /ˈpəʊst ˌɒfɪs/
postbox /ˈpəʊstbɒks/
to practise /ˈpræktɪs/
reservation /ˌrezəˈveɪʃn/
stairs /steəz/
stay (n) /steɪ/

Ordinal numbers
1st first /fɜːst/
2nd second /ˈsekənd/
3rd third /θɜːd/
4th fourth /fɔːθ/
5th fifth /fɪfθ/
6th sixth /sɪksθ/
7th seventh /ˈsevnθ/
8th eighth /eɪtθ/
9th ninth /naɪnθ/
10th tenth /tenθ/
11th eleventh /ɪˈlevnθ/
12th twelfth /twelfθ/
13th thirteenth /ˌθɜːˈtiːnθ/
14th fourteenth /ˌfɔːˈtiːnθ/
15th fifteenth /ˌfɪfˈtiːnθ/
16th sixteenth /ˌsɪksˈtiːnθ/
17th seventeenth /ˌsevnˈtiːnθ/
18th eighteenth /ˌeɪˈtiːnθ/
19th nineteenth /ˌnaɪnˈtiːnθ/
20th twentieth /ˈtwentiəθ/
21st twenty-first /ˌtwenti ˈfɜːst/
22nd twenty-second /ˌtwenti ˈsekənd/
30th thirtieth /ˈθɜːtiəθ/

Unit 8
Grammar
afraid (of) /əˈfreɪd/
ago /əˈgəʊ/
airport /ˈeəpɔːt/
alone /əˈləʊn/
asleep /əˈsliːp/
at home /ət ˈhəʊm/
at work /ət ˈwɜːk/
band /bænd/
to be away /ˌbiː əˈweɪ/
to be out /ˌbiː ˈaʊt/
brilliant /ˈbrɪliənt/
concert /ˈkɒnsət/
definitely /ˈdefnətli/
entertainment /ˌentəˈteɪnmənt/
the first time /ðə ˌfɜːst ˈtaɪm/
football match /ˈfʊtbɔːl ˌmætʃ/
imagination /ɪˌmædʒɪˈneɪʃn/
last Saturday /ˌlɑːst ˈsætədeɪ/
nil /nɪl/
noise /nɔɪz/
phone call /ˈfəʊn ˌkɔːl/
score /skɔː(r)/
someone /ˈsʌmwʌn/
something /ˈsʌmθɪŋ/
tired /ˈtaɪəd/
yesterday /ˈjestədeɪ/

Vocabulary
birthday /ˈbɜːθdeɪ/
date /deɪt/
month /mʌnθ/
wedding anniversary /ˈwedɪŋ ænɪˌvɜːsəri/

Months
January /ˈdʒænjuəri/
February /ˈfebruəri/
March /mɑːtʃ/
April /ˈeɪprəl/
May /meɪ/
June /dʒuːn/
July /dʒuˈlaɪ/
August /ˈɔːgəst/
September /sepˈtembə(r)/
October /ɒkˈtəʊbə(r)/
November /nəʊˈvembə(r)/
December /dɪˈsembə(r)/

Reading
aerobics /eəˈrəʊbɪks/
back /bæk/
calendar /ˈkælɪndə(r)/
class /klɑːs/
eagle /ˈiːgl/
to forget /fəˈget/
free /friː/
kick-off /ˈkɪk ˌɒf/
love (n) /lʌv/
next /nekst/
place /pleɪs/
play (n) /pleɪ/
special /ˈspeʃl/
surgeon /ˈsɜːdʒən/

Listening
all over the world /ˌɔːl ˌəʊvə ðə ˈwɜːld/
art /ɑːt/
at least /ət ˈliːst/

caravan /'kærəvæn/
Colombia /kə'lʌmbiə/
fantastic /fæn'tæstɪk/
hundreds /'hʌndrədz/
Japanese /ˌdʒæpə'ni:z/
Korea /kə'rɪə/
Mexican /'meksɪkən/
million /'mɪljən/
motor show /'məʊtə ˌʃəʊ/
music festival /'mju:zɪk ˌfestɪvl/
North African /ˌnɔ:θ 'æfrɪkən/
singer /'sɪŋə(r)/
tent /tent/
thousands /'θaʊzəndz/
Turkish /'tɜ:kɪʃ/
Uganda /ju:'gændə/

Weather
cloudy /'klaʊdi/
cold /kəʊld/
dry /draɪ/
sunny /'sʌni/
warm /wɔ:m/
weather /'weðə(r)/
wet /wet/
windy /'wɪndi/

Extension
Units 7 and 8
disk /dɪsk/
to hide /haɪd/
to laugh /lɑ:f/
to stare /steə(r)/
stereo /'steriəʊ/
to win /wɪn/
witness /'wɪtnəs/

Unit 9
Grammar
actress /'æktrəs/
alive /ə'laɪv/
ancestor /'ænsestə(r)/
to arrest /ə'rest/
to be born /ˌbi 'bɔ:n/
dangerous /'deɪndʒərəs/
to decide /dɪ'saɪd/
to die /daɪ/
either /'aɪðə(r)/
to escape /ɪ'skeɪp/
factory /'fæktri/
great-grandfather /ˌgreɪt 'grænfɑ:ðə(r)/
great-grandmother /ˌgreɪt 'grænmʌðə(r)/
imaginary /ɪ'mædʒɪnəri/
Ireland /'aɪələnd/
police /pə'li:s/
real /ri:l/
to remember /rɪ'membə(r)/
revolution /ˌrevə'lu:ʃn/
Russia /'rʌʃə/
to succeed /sək'si:d/
survivor /sə'vaɪvə(r)/

Vocabulary
to climb /klaɪm/
to cry /kraɪ/
to fall /fɔ:l/
to grab /græb/
to hold /həʊld/

to hurry /'hʌri/
to jump /dʒʌmp/
to lift /lɪft/
to look back /ˌlʊk 'bæk/
to look down /ˌlʊk 'daʊn/
to look up /ˌlʊk 'ʌp/
to slip /slɪp/
to talk /tɔ:k/
to wave /weɪv/
to whisper /'wɪspə(r)/

Reading
accident /'æksɪdənt/
as /æz, əz/
chairlift /'tʃeəlɪft/
coat /kəʊt/
excited /ɪk'saɪtɪd/
to follow /'fɒləʊ/
ground /graʊnd/
helicopter /'helɪkɒptə(r)/
hill /hɪl/
to hold on /ˌhəʊld 'ɒn/
just in time /ˌdʒʌst ɪn 'taɪm/
later /'leɪtə(r)/
lifetime /'laɪftaɪm/
metre /'mi:tə(r)/
New Zealand /ˌnju: 'zi:lənd/
operator /'ɒpəreɪtə(r)/
park (n) /pɑ:k/
to scream /skri:m/
second (n) /'sekənd/
to shout /ʃaʊt/
sky /skaɪ/
suddenly /'sʌdnli/
sunshine /'sʌnʃaɪn/
terror /'terə(r)/
theme park /'θi:m ˌpɑ:k/
to try /traɪ/
to wait for /'weɪt ˌfɔ:, fə(r)/
while /waɪl/

Prepositions of movement
above /ə'bʌv/
down /daʊn/
out of /'aʊt əv/
over /'əʊvə(r)/
round /raʊnd/
through /θru:/
up /ʌp/

Listening
to accept /ək'sept/
to add /æd/
a lot of /ə 'lɒt əv/
article /'ɑ:tɪkl/
to build /bɪld/
car park /'kɑ: ˌpɑ:k/
cottage /'kɒtɪdʒ/
to die out /ˌdaɪ 'aʊt/
dinosaur /'daɪnəsɔ:(r)/
to double /'dʌbl/
in fact /ˌɪn 'fækt/
to invite /ɪn'vaɪt/
to knock down /ˌnɒk 'daʊn/
land (n) /lænd/
not at all /ˌnɒt ət 'ɔ:l/
to offer /'ɒfə(r)/
plan (n) /plæn/
to plant /plɑ:nt/
to refuse /rɪ'fju:z/
reporter /rɪ'pɔ:tə(r)/
to sell /sel/
studio /'stju:diəʊ/

tree /tri:/
welcome /'welkəm/
What for? /ˌwɒt 'fɔ:/

Unit 10
Grammar
beach /bi:tʃ/
Bolivia /bə'lɪviə/
to break /breɪk/
couple /'kʌpl/
to guess /ges/
ill /ɪl/
journey /'dʒɜ:ni/
to lose /lu:z/
mountain /'maʊntɪn/
passport /'pɑ:spɔ:t/
Peru /pə'ru:/
sightseeing /'saɪtsi:ɪŋ/
to stay /steɪ/
wallet /'wɒlɪt/

Vocabulary
boarding pass /'bɔ:dɪŋ ˌpɑ:s/
to book /bʊk/
flight /flaɪt/
luggage /'lʌgɪdʒ/
to pack /pæk/
passenger /'pæsɪndʒə(r)/
platform /'plætfɔ:m/
return (n) /rɪ'tɜ:n/
seat /si:t/
single /'sɪŋgl/
suitcase /'su:tkeɪs/
travel agent /'trævl ˌeɪdʒənt/
traveller's cheques /'trævələz ˌtʃeks/
trolley /'trɒli/
visa /'vi:zə/

Reading
to ask /ɑ:sk/
to check out of /ˌtʃek 'aʊt əv/
coach /kəʊtʃ/
to direct /də'rekt/
embassy /'embəsi/
to fly /flaɪ/
frightened /'fraɪtənd/
to get on /ˌget 'ɒn/
to have a good time /ˌhæv ə ˌgʊd 'taɪm/
helpful /'helpfl/
interpreter /ɪn'tɜ:prɪtə(r)/
kind /kaɪnd/
professor /prə'fesə(r)/
pronunciation /prəˌnʌnsi'eɪʃn/
to provide /prə'vaɪd/
railway guard /'reɪlweɪ ˌgɑ:d/
to recognize /'rekəgnaɪz/
seaside /'si:saɪd/
to seem /si:m/
to set off /ˌset 'ɒf/
to sort out /ˌsɔ:t 'aʊt/
taxi /'tæksi/

Listening
a few /ə 'fju:/
accommodation /əˌkɒmə'deɪʃn/
adult /'ædʌlt/
business class /'bɪznɪs ˌklɑ:s/
direct /də'rekt/

economy class /ɪ'kɒnəmi ˌklɑ:s/
to stop over /ˌstɒp 'əʊvə(r)/
travel agency /'trævl ˌeɪdʒənsi/
whereabouts /'weərəbaʊts/

Extension
Units 9 and 10
beautiful /'bju:tɪfl/
castle /'kɑ:sl/
to get back /ˌget 'bæk/
guesthouse /'gesthaʊs/
to hire /'haɪə(r)/
to rain /reɪn/

Unit 11
Grammar
to carry /'kæri/
chemistry /'kemɪstri/
to come in /ˌkʌm 'ɪn/
fax machine /'fæks məˌʃi:n/
geography /dʒi'ɒgrəfi/
jeans /dʒi:nz/
to park /pɑ:k/
to put /pʊt/
still /stɪl/
to take off /ˌteɪk 'ɒf/
taxi driver /'tæksi ˌdraɪvə(r)/
to type /taɪp/
to wear /weə(r)/
well /wel/

Vocabulary
baseball cap /'beɪsbɔ:l ˌkæp/
clothes /kləʊðz/
coat /kəʊt/
gloves /glʌvz/
hat /hæt/
jacket /'dʒækɪt/
jumper /'dʒʌmpə(r)/
shirt /ʃɜ:t/
shoes /ʃu:z/
shorts /ʃɔ:ts/
skirt /skɜ:t/
socks /sɒks/
suit /su:t/
sweatshirt /'swetʃɜ:t/
tie /taɪ/
tights /taɪts/
top /tɒp/
trainers /'treɪnəz/
trousers /'traʊzəz/

Reading
across /ə'krɒs/
along /ə'lɒŋ/
best friend /ˌbest 'frend/
blouse /blaʊz/
bus stop /'bʌs ˌstɒp/
catwalk /'kætwɔ:k/
competition /ˌkɒmpə'tɪʃn/
contract /'kɒntrækt/
education /ˌedʒu'keɪʃn/
fashion /'fæʃn/
fashion show /'fæʃn ˌʃəʊ/
film star /'fɪlm ˌstɑ:(r)/
to flash /flæʃ/
future /'fju:tʃə(r)/
GCSE exams /ˌdʒi:si:es'i: ɪgˌzæmz/
homework /'həʊmwɜ:k/
latest /'leɪtɪst/
model /'mɒdl/

modelling agency /ˈmɒdlɪŋ ˌeɪdʒənsi/
nobody /ˈnəʊbədi/
playground /ˈpleɪɡraʊnd/
prize /praɪz/
quickly /ˈkwɪkli/
to take away /ˌteɪk əˈweɪ/
to think /θɪŋk/
uniform /ˈjuːnɪfɔːm/

Listening
certainly /ˈsɜːtnli/
changing room /ˈtʃeɪndʒɪŋ ˌruːm/
credit card /ˈkredɪt ˌkɑːd/
extra large /ˌekstrə ˈlɑːdʒ/
Just a minute. /ˌdʒʌst ə ˈmɪnɪt/
medium /ˈmiːdiəm/
nothing /ˈnʌθɪŋ/
of course /əv ˈkɔːs/
to sign /saɪn/
size /saɪz/
tracksuit /ˈtræksuːt/
to try on /ˌtraɪ ˈɒn/

Unit 12
Grammar
the best /ðə ˈbest/
better /ˈbetə(r)/
body /ˈbɒdi/
break (n) /breɪk/
difficult /ˈdɪfɪkəlt/
excellent /ˈeksələnt/
fit /fɪt/
happy /ˈhæpi/
health farm /ˈhelθ fɑːm/
healthy /ˈhelθi/
hobby /ˈhɒbi/
massage (n) /ˈmæsɑːʒ/
popular /ˈpɒpjələ(r)/
relaxed /rɪˈlækst/
to take exercise /ˌteɪk ˈeksəsaɪz/
test (n) /test/
worse /wɜːs/
the worst /ðə ˈwɜːst/

Seasons
spring /sprɪŋ/
summer /ˈsʌmə(r)/
autumn /ˈɔːtəm/
winter /ˈwɪntə(r)/

Vocabulary
arm /ɑːm/
chest /tʃest/
ear /ɪə(r)/
face /feɪs/
finger /ˈfɪŋɡə(r)/
foot /fʊt/
hand /hænd/
head /hed/
knee /niː/
leg /leɡ/
mouth /maʊθ/
neck /nek/
nose /nəʊz/
stomach /ˈstʌmək/
teeth /tiːθ/
thumb /θʌm/
toe /təʊ/

Reading
amazing /əˈmeɪzɪŋ/
to appear /əˈpɪə(r)/
to believe /bɪˈliːv/
bright /braɪt/
creature /ˈkriːtʃə(r)/
cut (n) /kʌt/
dirty /ˈdɜːti/
dream (n) /driːm/
each other /ˌiːtʃ ˈʌðə(r)/
to fall asleep /ˌfɔːl əˈsliːp/
huge /hjuːdʒ/
light (n) /laɪt/
to look out /ˌlʊk ˈaʊt/
naked /ˈneɪkɪd/
to notice /ˈnəʊtɪs/
object /ˈɒbdʒekt/
planet /ˈplænɪt/
to run away /ˌrʌn əˈweɪ/
the same /ðə ˈseɪm/
story /ˈstɔːri/
strange /streɪndʒ/
thought (n) /θɔːt/
universe /ˈjuːnɪvɜːs/
wheel /wiːl/
to worry /ˈwʌri/

Listening
back (n) /bæk/
cold (n) /kəʊld/
cough /kɒf/
fire /ˈfaɪə(r)/
headache /ˈhedeɪk/
hot /hɒt/
hungry /ˈhʌŋɡri/
to hurt /hɜːt/
optician's /ɒpˈtɪʃnz/
painkiller /ˈpeɪnkɪlə(r)/
to put on /ˌpʊt ˈɒn/
so much /ˌsəʊ ˈmʌtʃ/
sore throat /ˌsɔː ˈθrəʊt/
to stay up /ˌsteɪ ˈʌp/
stomach ache /ˈstʌmək ˌeɪk/
thirsty /ˈθɜːsti/
toothache /ˈtuːθeɪk/

Extension
Units 11 and 12
brain /breɪn/
Come on. /ˈkʌm ˌɒn/
crazy /ˈkreɪzi/
funny /ˈfʌni/
hospital /ˈhɒspɪtl/
medicine /ˈmedsn/
nervous /ˈnɜːvəs/
sore throat /ˌsɔː ˈθrəʊt/
terrible /ˈterəbl/

Unit 13
Grammar
album /ˈælbəm/
to change /tʃeɪndʒ/
charity /ˈtʃærəti/
congratulations /kənˌɡrætʃʊˈleɪʃnz/
equipment /ɪˈkwɪpmənt/
to give /ɡɪv/
Good idea. /ˌɡʊd aɪˈdɪə/
guitarist /ɡɪˈtɑːrɪst/
half /hɑːf/
to join /dʒɔɪn/
to kill /kɪl/
life /laɪf/

to look for /ˈlʊk ˌfɔː, fə(r)/
lottery /ˈlɒtəri/
millionaire /ˌmɪljəˈneə(r)/
national /ˈnæʃnəl/
overnight /ˌəʊvəˈnaɪt/
Speak for yourself. /ˌspiːk fə jəˈself/
to spend (money) /spend/
sports car /ˈspɔːts ˌkɑː(r)/
to tell /tel/
together /təˈgeðə(r)/
tour /ˈtʊə(r)/

Vocabulary
to call in /ˌkɔːl ˈɪn/
to call for /ˈkɔːl ˌfɔː, fə(r)/
to call up /ˌkɔːl ˈʌp/
dressing-gown /ˈdresɪŋ ˌɡaʊn/
to get to /ˈɡet ˌtuː, tə/
to go away /ˌɡəʊ əˈweɪ/
to look up (a word) /ˌlʊk ˈʌp/
to switch on /ˌswɪtʃ ˈɒn/
to take up /ˌteɪk ˈʌp/

Reading
army /ˈɑːmi/
as soon as /əz ˈsuːn əz/
ball /bɔːl/
to beat /biːt/
champion /ˈtʃæmpiən/
commentator /ˈkɒmənteɪtə(r)/
ever /ˈevə(r)/
golfer /ˈɡɒlfə(r)/
to go wild /ˌɡəʊ ˈwaɪld/
to hit /hɪt/
hole /həʊl/
junior /ˈdʒuːniə(r)/
keen /kiːn/
major /ˈmeɪdʒə(r)/
officer /ˈɒfɪsə(r)/
president /ˈprezɪdənt/
professional /prəˈfeʃnl/
several /ˈsevrəl/
Thailand /ˈtaɪlænd/
tiger /ˈtaɪɡə(r)/
tournament /ˈtʊənəmənt/

Listening
bowling alley /ˈbəʊlɪŋ ˌæli/
to get ready /ˌɡet ˈredi/
to give somebody a ring /ˌɡɪv ˌsʌmbədi ə ˈrɪŋ/
to go bowling /ˌɡəʊ ˈbəʊlɪŋ/
in town /ˌɪn ˈtaʊn/
local /ˈləʊkl/
to make a reservation /ˌmeɪk ə ˌrezəˈveɪʃn/
performance /pəˈfɔːməns/
phone book /ˈfəʊn ˌbʊk/
square (n) /skweə(r)/
to suggest /səˈdʒest/
suggestion /səˈdʒestʃən/
tonight /təˈnaɪt/

Unit 14
Grammar
adventure /ədˈventʃə(r)/
advert /ˈædvɜːt/
art gallery /ˈɑːt ˌɡæləri/
bone /bəʊn/
canoeing /kəˈnuːɪŋ/

detail /ˈdiːteɪl/
eclipse /ɪˈklɪps/
hang-gliding /ˈhæŋ ˌɡlaɪdɪŋ/
horror movie /ˈhɒrə ˌmuːvi/
kilt /kɪlt/
noisy /ˈnɔɪzi/
racing car /ˈreɪsɪŋ ˌkɑː(r)/
scuba-diving /ˈskuːbə ˌdaɪvɪŋ/
twice /twaɪs/

Vocabulary
bridge /brɪdʒ/
field /fiːld/
forest /ˈfɒrɪst/
island /ˈaɪlənd/
lake /leɪk/
river /ˈrɪvə(r)/
road /rəʊd/
sea /siː/
valley /ˈvæli/

Continents
Africa /ˈæfrɪkə/
Asia /ˈeɪʒə/
Australasia /ˌɒstrəˈleɪʒə/
Europe /ˈjʊərəp/
North America /ˌnɔːθ əˈmerɪkə/
South America /ˌsaʊθ əˈmerɪkə/

Points of the compass
north /nɔːθ/
south /saʊθ/
east /iːst/
west /west/

Reading
ancient /ˈeɪnʃənt/
bird /bɜːd/
civilization /ˌsɪvəlaɪˈzeɪʃn/
to count /kaʊnt/
data /ˈdeɪtə/
to dig up /ˌdɪɡ ˈʌp/
to disappear /ˌdɪsəˈpɪə(r)/
elephant /ˈelɪfənt/
expedition /ˌekspəˈdɪʃn/
to explore /ɪkˈsplɔː(r)/
female /ˈfiːmeɪl/
male /meɪl/
ordinary /ˈɔːdnri/
organization /ˌɔːɡənaɪˈzeɪʃn/
to photograph /ˈfəʊtəɡrɑːf/
rain forest /ˈreɪn ˌfɒrɪst/
to study /ˈstʌdi/
volunteer /ˌvɒlənˈtɪə(r)/
whale /weɪl/

Listening
lucky /ˈlʌki/
lucky break /ˌlʌki ˈbreɪk/
quiz show /ˈkwɪz ˌʃəʊ/
surprised /səˈpraɪzd/
presenter /prɪˈzentə(r)/

Extension
Units 13 and 14
character /ˈkærəktə(r)/
to interview /ˈɪntəvjuː/
to invent /ɪnˈvent/
soap opera /ˈsəʊp ˌɒprə/

Tapescripts

1.3
Paolo Hi. I'm Paolo.
Banu Nice to meet you, Paolo. My name's Banu.
Paolo Pleased to meet you, Banu. Where are you from?
Banu I'm from Turkey. And you?
Paolo I'm from Italy.

1.4
Gábor Hi. My name's Gábor.
Michael Pleased to meet you, Gábor. I'm Michael and this is Sarah.
Sarah Where are you from, Gábor?
Gábor I'm from Hungary. And you?
Sarah We're from the USA.

Keiko Hi. I'm from Japan. My name is Keiko.
Telma Pleased to meet you, Keiko. I'm Telma.
Keiko And what's your name?
Fernando My name's Fernando.
Keiko Nice to meet you. Where are you from?
Fernando We're from Brazil.

1.6
1 **A** What's your phone number?
  B It's 0181 463 9865.
  A Can you repeat that, please?
  B Yes. It's 0181 …
  A 0181 …
  B 463 …
  A 463 …
  B 9865.
  A 9865. Thank you.
2 So, the number is 01765 36119.
  That's 01765 36119.
3 **A** This is my new phone number.
    It's 512090.
  B 512090?
  A Yes.
4 Call this number now: 0898 44 33 88.
  That's 0898 44 33 88.

1.7
1 Turn to page 61. That's page 61.
2 **A** How old are you?
  B I'm 16.
3 **A** Is this room 53?
  B No, it isn't. This is room 42.
  A Oh, thank you.
4 **A** What number is your house?
  B It's number 80.
  A 18?
  B No, 80 – eight oh.
  A Oh, right.
5 **A** Here you are Mrs Clark. You're in Room 79.
  B 79. Thank you.

1.9
1 is an umbrella. That's U-M-B-R-E-double L-A. Umbrella.
2 is a teacher. That's T-E-A-C-H-E-R. Teacher.
3 is a man. That's M-A-N. Man.
4 is a woman. That's W-O-M-A-N. Woman.
5 is a girl. That's G-I-R-L. Girl.
6 is a boy. That's B-O-Y. Boy.
7 is a pen. That's P-E-N. Pen.
8 is an apple. That's A-double P-L-E. Apple.
9 is a desk. That's D-E-S-K. Desk.
10 is an orange. That's O-R-A-N-G-E. Orange.
11 is a book. That's B-double O-K. Book.
12 is a bag. That's B-A-G. Bag.
13 is a notebook. That's N-O-T-E-B-O-O-K. Notebook.
14 is a student. That's S-T-U-D-E-N-T. Student.

1.11
Receptionist OK. Now, what's your name?
Mandy It's Mandy Wallis.
Receptionist How do you spell Wallis?
Mandy It's W-A-double L-I-S.
Receptionist W-A-double L-I-S. Thank you. And how old are you?
Mandy I'm nineteen.
Receptionist What's your address?
Mandy It's 14 Kent Street, Lancaster, LA2 6NV.
Receptionist I'm sorry, is that 14 or 40?
Mandy 14. One four.
Receptionist Thank you. And what's your telephone number?
Mandy It's 01524 694817.
Receptionist Can you repeat that, please?
Mandy Yes. 01524 …
Receptionist 01524 …
Mandy 694817.
Receptionist 694817. Thank you.

1.14
1 The fast car is red.
2 The brown shoes are old.
3 The expensive hat is yellow.
4 The black and white dog is big.
5 The new shoes are blue.
6 The red car is slow.
7 The small dog is white.
8 The cheap hat is green.

1.15
1 **Assistant** Yes, please?
  Customer Two hot dogs, please.
  Assistant Anything else?
  Customer No, thank you.
  Assistant That's £5.20, please.
  Customer Thank you.
2 **Assistant** Yes, please?
  Customer A hamburger and a lemonade, please.
  Assistant Small or large?
  Customer Small, please.
  Assistant That's £4, please.
  Customer Thank you.
3 **Assistant** Yes, please?
  Customer A large coffee, please.
  Assistant Anything else?
  Customer No, thanks.
  Assistant 70p, please.
  Customer Thank you.

1.16
one pound twenty
seventy-five pence
sixty-four pence
nine pounds
nine pounds forty-five
one pound fifteen
twelve pence
ninety-nine pence

2.2
Open your notebook.
Pick up your pen.
Write your name.
Don't write your address.
Close your notebook.
Don't put your notebook in your bag.
Stand up.
Pick up your book.

Turn to page 8.
Look at exercise 3.
Read exercise 3.
Don't close your book.
Don't sit down.
Turn to your partner.
Say *Hello*.
Don't look at the board.
Look at your teacher.
Look at your bag.
Sit down.
Thank you!

2.4
student
waiter
waitress
shop assistant
doctor
teacher
bank clerk
secretary
architect
dentist
engineer
nurse
pilot

2.5
Melanie Hi, Jason. How are you?
Jason I'm fine thanks. And you?
Melanie Fine. Who's that guy over there?
Jason Oh. That's Ken. He's from Australia.
Melanie Mmm. He's rather nice.
Jason Yes, he is, but …
Barry Jason! How are you?
Jason Oh, hello, Barry. I'm fine.
Melanie See you, Jason.
Jason Oh, yes. Bye, Melanie.

Melanie Hello, I'm Melanie.
Ken How do you do, Melanie? I'm Ken.
Melanie Nice to meet you. Are you from Australia?
Ken Yes, I am. I'm from Sydney.
Melanie Oh, that's nice. What do you do?
Ken I'm an architect. What about you?
Melanie I'm a nurse.
Ken Oh, that's interesting. My wife's a nurse, too.
Melanie Your wife?
Ken Yes, just a minute. Maria?
Maria Yes.
Ken Melanie, this is my wife, Maria. Melanie's a nurse, too.
Maria Pleased to meet you, Melanie.
Melanie Yes, nice to meet you, too.
Ken Are you …

2.6
1 **A** Hello, I'm Barry.
  B How do you do, Barry? I'm Maria.
  A Pleased to meet you. What do you do?
  B I'm a nurse.
  A That's interesting.
  B What about you?
  A I'm an engineer.
  B Where are you from?
  A I'm from Canada.
2 **A** Hi. How are you?
  B I'm fine, thanks. And you?
  A Oh, not bad. How are the kids?
  B They're all fine.
  A Well, I must be off. See you.
  B Yes, bye.

Extension Units 1 and 2

Receptionist Good morning.

Martina Hello. I'm a new student.

Receptionist Well, welcome to the Gordon Language School! Now, you need to have an interview first. That's in room 16.

Martina I'm sorry. Can you repeat that, please?

Receptionist Yes, of course. Go to room 16.

Martina Room 16?

Receptionist Yes. It's over there.

Martina Thank you.

Paul Come in.

Martina Hello. I'm a new student.

Paul Oh, right. Well, come in and sit down. What's your name?

Martina It's Martina. Martina Echevarría.

Paul Pleased to meet you, Martina. I'm Paul Barton.

Martina How do you do? Are you a teacher here?

Paul Yes, I am. Well, we just need to complete the form first. Now, it's Martina. Is that M-A-R-T-I-N-A?

Martina Yes, that's right.

Paul And how do you spell your surname? Eche, er …

Martina Echevarría. It's E-C-H-E-V …

Paul E-C-H-E-V … Yes …

Martina A-double R-I-A.

Paul A-double R-I-A. Thank you. And where are you from?

Martina I'm from Argentina.

Paul How old are you?

Martina I'm twenty.

Paul And what do you do?

Martina I'm sorry. I don't understand.

Paul Oh, er, what do you do? What's your job?

Martina Job? Oh, I'm a student.

Paul And what's your address?

Martina My address? In Argentina?

Paul No, your address here in London.

Martina Oh, it's 62 Canada Street.

Paul 62 Canada Street. Like the country? Canada?

Martina Yes. And that's London SW12 …

Paul SW12 …

Martina 7TH.

Paul 7TH. And your telephone number?

Martina It's 0181 764 8943.

Paul 0181 764 8943. Thank you. Right, well, now …

3.2

1 He's got blue eyes. He's got short, fair hair. He's got a moustache.

2 He's got brown eyes. He's bald. He's got a beard.

3 She's got green eyes. She's got long, dark hair. She's got glasses.

3.3

brother
sister
son
daughter
father
mother
uncle
aunt
nephew
niece
cousin
cousin
grandfather
grandmother
grandson
granddaughter

3.4

Shop assistant Good afternoon. Can I help you?

Customer Yes. How much is this black T-shirt?

Shop assistant It's £10.50.

Customer And how much are those watches over there?

Shop assistant They're £7.25 each.

Customer Well, can I have this T-shirt, please?

Shop assistant Certainly.

Customer And that red watch with the blue strap.

Shop assistant This one?

Customer Yes, that's it. And have you got any postcards?

Shop assistant Yes, they're over there. They're 50p each.

Customer I'll have these two, please.

Shop assistant Certainly. Anything else?

Customer No, thank you.

Shop assistant Right, well, that will be £18.75 altogether.

Customer Here you are.

Shop assistant Thank you. That's £1.25 change.

Customer Thank you. Goodbye.

Shop assistant Goodbye.

4.2

1 **Interviewer** What's your name?

Sarah It's Sarah Ballard.

Interviewer How do you spell Ballard?

Sarah It's B-A-double L-A-R-D.

Interviewer Thank you. Now, can you drive, Sarah?

Sarah Well, I haven't got a car, but I can drive.

Interviewer Can you play a musical instrument?

Sarah No, not really.

Interviewer Can you speak any foreign languages?

Sarah Yes, I can speak French quite well.

Interviewer Can you cook?

Sarah Yes, I can.

Interviewer Can you play any sports?

Sarah No, I don't really like sport.

Interviewer Can you swim?

Sarah Yes, I can.

Interviewer Thank you, Sarah.

2 **Interviewer** What's your name?

Tony It's Tony Cooke.

Interviewer How do you spell Cooke? Has it got an E?

Tony Yes. C-double O-K-E.

Interviewer Thanks. Now, can you drive, Tony?

Tony Yes, I can.

Interviewer Can you play a musical instrument?

Tony Yes, I can play the saxophone.

Interviewer Can you speak any foreign languages?

Tony Yes, German and Spanish.

Interviewer Can you cook?

Tony No, I never cook!

Interviewer Can you play any sports?

Tony Yes, I can play football, tennis, golf, and rugby.

Interviewer Can you swim?

Tony No, I can't.

Interviewer Thank you, Tony.

4.3

sports
golf
basketball
rugby

activities
ride a bicycle
swim
ski
drive a car
dance
run
ride a horse
sing
paint

musical instruments
violin
drums
saxophone

4.4

1 three o'clock
2 five past ten
3 ten past six
4 quarter past eleven
5 twenty past eight
6 twenty-five past nine
7 half past one
8 twenty-five to four
9 twenty to two
10 quarter to seven
11 ten to twelve
12 five to five

4.5

1 A What's the time?
B It's five past three.

2 A Can we meet on Monday at half past nine?
B Can we make it quarter to ten?
A Yes, OK.

3 Good afternoon. This is Radio BGK. It's twenty-five to four.

4 A Can I make an appointment with the dentist, please?
B Yes. Can you come at twenty past eleven on Thursday?
A Yes, that's fine.

5 A Is that conference in the morning?
B Yes, from nine o'clock to half past twelve.

6 A What about a game of golf on Sunday?
B OK. I can be there at quarter past eight.
A Fine.

7 A What time do I have to meet those visitors?
B At ten to two.
A Thanks.

4.7

1 A Is the meeting on Friday?
B Yes, that's right. It's at 3.30 in room 20.

2 A Is the conference on a weekday?
B No, it isn't. It's on Saturday morning.
A Oh, no. I can't go at the weekend.

3 A I've got an appointment at the doctor's on Wednesday.
B Is it in the afternoon?
A No, it's in the evening.

4 A Is your plane at 11.00 in the morning?
B No, it's at 11.00 at night.

4.8

1 **Jenny** Hello. Jenny Mills.

Secretary Hello, Jenny. I've got the manager for you.

Jenny Oh, OK.

Manager Jenny. We've got a bit of a problem. Can you go to the BAC conference on Tuesday?

Jenny The BAC conference? Can't Stephen go?

121

Manager No, I'm afraid he can't. He has to go to Spain on Monday night.

Jenny Oh, well. Just a minute. Tuesday? Yes, that's OK.

Manager Good. Thanks very much, Jenny.

2 **Jenny** Hello.

Mark Hello, Jenny?

Jenny Oh, hi Mark.

Mark Look, I'm afraid I can't make our meeting today. I have to finish a report. Can we meet on Wednesday afternoon?

Jenny No, I'm sorry. I have to go to the dentist's.

Mark Oh, and Thursday's no good for me. What about Friday?

Jenny In the afternoon?

Mark No, in the morning. Is 10.30 OK for you?

Jenny Yes, it's fine.

Mark Thanks. Well, I must be off. See you on Friday.

Jenny Yes. See you.

3 **Jenny** Hello. 84932.

Sylvia Hi Jenny. It's Sylvia.

Jenny Oh, hi Sylvia. How are you?

Sylvia Fine, thanks. Listen. Can you play tennis at the weekend, Jen?

Jenny Well, I can't play on Saturday. I have to go to London. But Sunday's OK for me. What about Sunday evening at about 6.00?

Sylvia No. Six is no good for me. Can we make it 7.30?

Jenny Yes, that's OK. Seven thirty's all right for me. Anyway, how are things …

📼 Extension Units 3 and 4

Receptionist Good morning. Can I help you?

Mr Smith Yes, can I make an appointment with Doctor Wall, please?

Receptionist Yes. Can you come at ten to three on Wednesday afternoon?

Mr Smith No, I'm sorry. I can't. What about the evening?

Receptionist Doctor Wall isn't here in the evening on Wednesday, I'm afraid. I can put you in at half past six on Thursday evening.

Mr Smith Yes, that's fine.

Receptionist What name is it, please?

Mr Smith It's Tom Smith.

Receptionist Thank you, Mr Smith. Goodbye.

Mr Smith Goodbye.

📼 Extension (Units 3 and 4)

Wild Thing

Wild Thing,
You make my heart sing.
You make everything move, baby.
Wild Thing.
Wild Thing, I think I love you,
But I want to know for sure.
Ah come on and hold me tight.
I love you.

📼 5.2

Meat
bacon
sausages
Drinks
beer
water
wine
milk
Fruit
bananas
grapes

Vegetables
mushrooms
potatoes
tomatoes
Other
pasta
fish
cheese
sandwiches
rice
eggs
bread

📼 5.4

1 **A** What would you like to drink?

B I'll have a cup of tea, please.

A A cup of tea and an orange juice, please.

C Do you want milk and sugar in the tea?

B Just milk, please.

C That's £1.80, please.

A Here you are.

C Thank you.

2 **A** Would you like a drink?

B Yes, please. I'll have a glass of wine.

A Red or white?

B Red, please.

A A glass of red wine, please. And I'll have a lemonade.

C Do you want ice in the lemonade?

A No, thank you.

C That's £3.40, please.

A Here you are.

C Thank you.

3 **A** Do you want a drink?

B Oh yes. I'll have a black coffee, please.

A A black coffee, please. And a glass of milk.

C Do you want sugar in the coffee?

B No, thank you.

C That's £1.40, please.

A Here you are.

C Thank you.

📼 5.5

1 Do you like tennis?

2 Would you like a game of tennis?

3 Would you like a glass of wine?

4 Do you like Oasis?

5 Would you like to dance?

6 Do you like red wine?

7 Do you like dancing?

8 Do you like having a big breakfast?

9 Would you like a cup of coffee?

10 Would you like to go to the shops?

📼 5.6

come
long
the
niece
fax
badge
watch
you

📼 6.1

1 **A** Hello, Transport Museum.

B Oh, hello. What time does the museum open today, please?

A It opens at ten o'clock.

B Thank you.

2 **A** Hello, ABC Cinema.

B Oh, hello. What time does the film start this evening, please?

A Which film – *The Winner* or *Monday, Monday*?

B Oh, *Monday, Monday*, please.

A That's in Studio 2 and it starts at seven forty-five.

B Thank you.

3 **A** What time does the train leave?

B The London train?

A Yes.

B Er, just a minute. It leaves in fifteen minutes, at ten past eleven.

A Ten past eleven. Thank you.

4 **A** I have to go out at eight. What time does this programme finish?

B Oh, I don't know. Just a minute, it's in the newspaper here. Er, it finishes at quarter past eight.

A Oh, well can you record it for me, please?

B OK.

A Thanks.

5 **A** What time do the shops close on Tuesdays?

B They close at five thirty, I think.

A Thank you.

6 **A** What time does your parents' plane arrive this afternoon?

B It arrives at two twenty.

A Twenty past two. Can you meet them?

B Yes, I can.

7 **A** What time do lessons finish today?

B They finish at ten to one.

A Ten to one? OK, thanks,

8 **A** What time does the supermarket close?

B Six thirty, I think. Oh no, just a minute. It's Friday today, so it closes at half past eight.

A Oh good. I can go after work. Thanks.

📼 Extension Units 5 and 6

Interviewer It's time now for *Lifestyles*. This is the part of the programme when we talk to ordinary people about their daily lives. Our guest in the studio today is Saul Robbins. Welcome to the programme, Saul.

Saul Thank you. It's nice to be here.

Interviewer Well, Saul, can I ask you some questions? First, where do you live?

Saul I live in New York. I don't come from the USA. I come from Canada, but I live in the US now.

Interviewer Do you like New York?

Saul Oh yes, it's a great city.

Interviewer And what do you do there?

Saul I'm a reporter.

Interviewer Where do you work?

Saul I work for a newspaper.

Interviewer So I suppose you don't work normal office hours? What time do you usually go to work?

Saul I leave home at about five o'clock in the afternoon.

Interviewer Really? So what time do you get up?

Saul Oh, usually about midday or 1.00.

Interviewer What do you do first when you get up?

Saul Oh, I always have a shower first.

Interviewer And what do you have for breakfast?

Saul I never eat breakfast. I just have a cup of coffee.

Interviewer How do you travel to work?

Saul Well, I live near the office, so I walk.

Interviewer And when do you finish work?

Saul I usually finish at two o'clock in the morning. I sometimes have to stay till four or five, if there's a big story, but it's usually about two o'clock.

Interviewer And what do you do after work?

Saul Oh, I usually go for a drink with some of the other people at the office.

Interviewer Do you travel to other countries with your job?

Saul No, I don't. I sometimes travel to other parts of the US, but not to other countries.

Interviewer Do you like your job?

Saul Yes, I love it! It's very interesting.

Interviewer And what do you do in your free time?

Saul Free time? Oh, I play tennis every day.

Interviewer Thank you, Saul.

7.1

1 How many people are there in the room?
2 How many books are there on the desk?
3 Are there any photographs on the desk?
4 Is there a musical instrument in the room?
5 How many boxes are there in the cupboard?
6 What is there on the floor next to the armchair?
7 Is there a telephone on the desk?
8 Where is the cat?
9 Are there any books on the floor?
10 Is there anything under the desk?

7.2

1 A Good evening, Madam.
  B Good evening. Do you have a reservation in the name of Mrs Gonzalez, please?
  A Just a moment, Madam. Yes, here you are. You're in room 732. That's on the seventh floor. The lifts are behind you.
  B Thank you.
  A Enjoy your stay.
2 A Hello. Where can we get some bread for breakfast in the morning, please?
  B In the shop. It's the second building on the right over there.
  A What time does it open?
  B At 6.30.
  A Thank you.
3 A Excuse me. Where's the toilet, please?
  B It's the third door on the left.
  A Third door on the left? Thank you.
4 A Hello, can I help you?
  B Hello. Is there a post office here, please?
  A Yes, sir. It's on the first floor, but I'm afraid it's closed now.
  B Is there a postbox there?
  A Yes, sir, and you can buy stamps from the machine.
  B Thank you.
  A You're welcome.
5 A Good morning. Can I help you?
  B Good morning. Where can I find Mrs Wilson of Redland Holdings, please?
  A Mrs Wilson is in room 2654.
  B 2654? Is that on the second floor?
  A No, it's on the twenty-sixth floor.
  B Oh, I see! Thank you.
6 A Excuse me. Where can I find Johnson's camera shop?
  B Johnson's? It's on the third level. Take the escalator up to the third level. When you get off the escalator it's on the right.
  A Thank you.

7.6

1 It's twenty to three in the afternoon.
2 There are two armchairs in the living room.
3 Would you like a cup of tea?
4 My bedroom's at the back of the house.
5 Do you like listening to music?
6 What time does the programme finish?

7 Can you make a game of tennis on Saturday?
8 Do you want to go out?
9 I'm afraid that's no good for me.
10 Are you the director of this film?

8.1

Peter

Checkout assistant That's £67.14, please.

Peter Oh, er, here you are.

Checkout assistant Thank you.

Mr and Mrs Williams

Mr Williams I like this part. It's my favourite.

Mrs Williams Ssh!

Mr Williams Sorry.

Mrs Williams Ssh!

Maria

Doctor Maria Jarvis, please.

Maria Good morning.

Doctor Good morning. What's the problem?

Maria Well, I can't move my arm and my back hurts.

Doctor Oh dear. Well, let's have a look at you.

Ben and Conny

Ben Go on! Shoot!

Zach and Hanna

Go hence, to have more talk of these sad things.
Some shall be pardoned, and some punished;
For never was a story of more woe
Than that of Juliet and her Romeo.

Ian

Dentist Open wide.

Mrs Vinney

A This is the end for you, McGee.
B Oh, no, it isn't.

Mr Ferreira

Final call for Cathay Pacific flight CX270 to Hong Kong. Please proceed to gate 24.

Fawzia and Samir

The train now at platform 2 is for Birmingham New Street, calling at Banbury, Leamington Spa, Coventry, Birmingham International, and Birmingham New Street. Platform 2 for the 3.45 to Birmingham New Street.

the Parkers

Father Dinner's ready.

Boy Can we watch television?

Mother No, you can't.

Boy Oh!

8.3

1 A What's the date today?
  B It's the fifteenth of March.
  A Thanks.
2 A When was Mark and Paula's party? Was it in May or June?
  B It was on the thirty-first of May, I think.
3 A When's your birthday?
  B It's on October the twenty-second.
4 A What was the date last Saturday?
  B Well, it's the fourth of February today, so Saturday was, er, the twenty-eighth of January.
  A Thanks.
5 A Is that film still on at the cinema?
  B Yes, it's on till September the nineteenth.
  A Good.
6 A What are the dates of our holiday?
  B From the twenty-first of July to the third of August.
  A Oh, right. Thanks.

8.4

Ben Hi, Karen.

Karen Hello, Ben. How are you?

Ben I'm fine, thanks. And you?

Karen Fine.

Ben Were you and Josh away at the weekend?

Karen Yes, we were at WOMAD.

Ben WOMAD? What's that?

Karen Oh, it's a music festival. World of Music, Arts, and Dance.

Ben Oh, I see. Where was that?

Karen It was in Reading.

Ben Oh, right. Was it good?

Karen Yes, it was fantastic. There were bands and singers from all over the world. My favourite band was from Uganda. They were so good. And there was lots of wonderful food – Indian, North African, Mexican, Japanese.

Ben Were there many people there?

Karen Yes, thousands.

Ben It sounds great.

Karen Yes, it was – apart from the weather!

Ben Why? What was the weather like?

Karen Wet.

Ben Oh, really? It wasn't too bad here. It was a bit cloudy, but it was dry.

Karen Well, it was OK on Saturday morning in Reading, too. It wasn't very sunny, but it was quite warm. But then the rest of the time it was very wet, and cold, too.

Ben Oh, that's a pity.

Karen Yes, but at least we were in a caravan, so we were all right, but a lot of people were in tents, so it wasn't very nice for them.

Ben No, I bet it wasn't. Were you there all weekend?

Karen Yes, from Friday evening till Sunday evening. And how was your weekend?

Ben Oh, it was OK. I was at …

8.5

1	his	his
2	these	this
3	he's	he's
4	his	he's
5	these	these
6	this	this
7	this	these
8	he's	his

Extension Units 7 and 8

It was half past ten. The date was Thursday the twenty-second of June. There were three other customers in the shop – two men and a woman. One of the men was bald. The woman was tall and thin and her hair was blond. The door of the manager's office was open and the manager was in his office. He was on the telephone. There were two shop assistants. One assistant was with the woman. There were some rings on the counter. The door of the shop was open. In front of the shop there was a blue car. Its registration number was R593 KBJ. Near the car there was a man with a small black dog.

Extension Units 7 and 8

You've got to hide your love away

Here I stand, head in hand,
Turn my face to the wall.
If she's gone I can't go on,
Feeling two foot small.
Everywhere people stare,
Each and every day,
I can see them laugh at me,
And I hear them say,
Hey, you've got to hide your love away.
Hey, you've got to hide your love away.

How can I even try?
I can never win.
Hearing them and seeing them,
In the state I'm in.
How can she say to me,
'Love will find a way'?
Gather round all you clowns,
Let me hear you say,
Hey, you've got to hide your love away.
Hey, you've got to hide your love away.

📼 **9.2**

Adam This is my great-grandmother, Sheena.
Madelaine Was she born in the USA?
Adam No, she wasn't. She was born in Ireland.
Madelaine When did her family move to the States?
Adam Her parents moved there when Sheena was still a child.
Madelaine Why did they decide to leave Ireland?
Adam They wanted to find a better life.
Madelaine Where did they live in the USA?
Adam They lived in New York when they first arrived.
Madelaine Did they stay there?
Adam Her parents did, but Sheena decided to go to Hollywood.
Madelaine Did she want to work in films?
Adam Yes, she wanted to be an actress.
Madelaine Did she succeed?
Adam No, she didn't. Then she married my great-grandfather, Alexei.
Madelaine Did she die before you were born?
Adam No, she didn't. She died when she was 96, so I can remember her.

📼 **9.3**

Interviewer In the studio today we have Eileen Halliday. Eileen lives at Riverside Cottage. Two years ago Sainsbury's, the supermarket company, wanted to buy her land and knock down her cottage. But 79-year-old Eileen didn't like that idea at all.
Interviewer Welcome to the studio, Eileen.
Eileen Hello.
Interviewer Why did Sainsbury's want to buy your land?
Eileen They wanted to build a car park for their new supermarket.
Interviewer How much money did they offer you?
Eileen They offered me £125,000.
Interviewer Did you accept it?
Eileen No, I didn't!
Interviewer So what did they do then?
Eileen They doubled it to £250,000 and they added a holiday, too.
Interviewer What did you say to that?
Eileen Well, I refused that, too.
Interviewer But that's a lot of money. Why did you refuse it?
Eileen What do I want all that money for? I'm 79 years old, and I haven't got any children. I just wanted to stay in my own home.
Interviewer So what did Sainsbury's do?
Eileen Well, they just accepted it and changed their plans.
Interviewer Did you have any problems after that?
Eileen No, I didn't, and they planted some nice trees between my cottage and the car park.
Interviewer Do you shop at the supermarket now?
Eileen Yes, I do. In fact I was their first customer. The manager invited me to open the new supermarket.

Interviewer Did you enjoy that?
Eileen Oh yes, I did. The newspapers and the television companies were all there. It was wonderful!

📼 **10.1**

Matt Hi, Dad.
Father Hello, Matt. How are you?
Matt I'm fine, thanks. We're in Bolivia now.
Father Did you have a good time in Peru?
Matt Yes, we did.
Father We got your postcard last week. How long did you spend there?
Matt We were there for about three weeks.
Father What did you do?
Matt Oh, we visited lots of places.
Father Did you find good places to stay?
Matt Yes, we didn't have any problems. But guess what. I lost my wallet.
Father Oh no! How did that happen?
Matt I left it on the beach.
Father Did you find it again?
Matt No, I didn't. We went back to look for it, but we didn't find it. But it was OK. There wasn't much in it. My passport and tickets and money were all at the hotel …

📼 **10.2**

1 **Travel agent** Good morning. Can I help you?
Customer Yes. I have to go to Moscow for a few days on 2 March.
Travel agent On 2 March. And when do you want to come back?
Customer Returning on 6 March.
Travel agent Is it just for yourself?
Customer Yes, it is.
Travel agent Do you need accommodation, too?
Customer Yes, please. I'd like a hotel near the centre of the city.
Travel agent And do you want to fly business class or economy?
Customer Can you give me prices for both, please?
Travel agent Yes, of course. Well, let's just have a look at the computer …

2 **Travel agent** Hello. How can I help?
Customer Hello. We'd like to book a flight to Australia, please.
Travel agent Yes, of course. Whereabouts in Australia?
Customer Sydney, please.
Travel agent Sydney, Australia. And when do you want to go?
Customer In the second week of November.
Travel agent And how long do you want to go for?
Customer For two months.
Travel agent Is it for two people?
Customer Yes, please. Myself and my husband.
Travel agent And do you need accommodation?
Customer 2 No, thank you. Our son and his wife live out there.
Travel agent Oh, I see. Now do you want to fly direct or would you like to stop over somewhere on the way?
Customer 2 Oh, er, how long is the flight?
Travel agent It's about 24 hours. So a lot of people stop over in Singapore, Bangkok, or Hong Kong.
Customer 2 Oh, I see. Well can you give us information for a direct flight and with a stopover in Singapore, please?

Travel agent Yes, OK. Let's see. Sydney in November. Now …

3 **Travel agent** Hi. Can I help you?
Customer Yes, we'd like to book a trip to Italy, please.
Travel agent I see. How long do you want to go for?
Customer We want to spend about two weeks there.
Travel agent And when do you want to travel?
Customer Next weekend.
Travel agent Next weekend? And how would you like to go?
Customer We'd like to go by train or by coach.
Customer 2 Oh, come on, Kelly. Why don't we go by plane?
Customer Look. You know I don't like flying. We talked about all this yesterday.
Customer 3 But the coach takes so long.
Customer Yes, but it's cheap and we can see things on the way. No, train or coach, please.
Travel agent How many people is it for?
Customer Three.
Travel agent All adults?
Customer 2 Well, we are, but Kelly isn't.
Customer Oh, very funny. Yes, all adults.
Travel agent And do you need accommodation?
Customer Yes, a hotel, but not too expensive.
Travel agent OK. Well we haven't got a lot for next weekend, but I can have a look for you. Just a minute and I'll …

📼 **Extension** Units 9 and 10

1 **William** Hi, Julia. Did you have a good holiday?
Julia Yes, thanks. It was very nice.
William Where did you go?
Julia We went to Scotland.
William Oh yes? Whereabouts were you?
Julia We were in Edinburgh.
William Very nice. How long were you there for?
Julia Just a week, but we wanted to stay longer!
William What was the weather like?
Julia Well, it rained for the first couple of days, but after that it was OK. It was cloudy, but it was dry.
William That's not too bad. Did you drive?
Julia No, we didn't. We don't like driving long distances, so we went by train.
William How long did the journey take?
Julia Oh, about five hours, I think. We got to Edinburgh at about 7.00 in the evening.
William Did you stay in a hotel?
Julia No, we didn't. We stayed with some friends. They've got a new flat in the city centre.
William Oh, right. What things did you do?
Julia We did quite a lot. We visited the castle and places like that. And we did a lot of shopping, too!
William Great. So when did you get back?
Julia Two days ago.
William Well, nice to see you again. See you around.
Julia OK. See you.

2 **Penny** Hi, David. How was your holiday?
David It was great, thanks.
Penny Good. When did you get back?

David We got back last Sunday.
Penny Where did you go?
David We went to Spain.
Penny Very nice. How long were you away? Was it just a week?
David No, two weeks.
Penny Did you fly?
David No, we didn't. We went by car.
Penny Oh, really? How long did that take?
David About two days, but we stopped in a few places in France on the way.
Penny Where did you stay?
David We stayed in hotels and guesthouses.
Penny Was the weather nice?
David It was fine for the first week – warm and sunny. After that it was a bit cool, but it didn't rain, so it was OK.
Penny What things did you do?
David Well, we spent the first few days on the beach, but we did some sightseeing too. In the second week we drove up into the mountains. It was beautiful up there, really quiet and peaceful, and no tourists!
Penny Great! Well, I'm glad you had a good time.
David Thanks. Anyway, how are things here?
Penny Oh, much the same, you know …

11.1

1 **Assistant** Can I help you?
Customer Yes. How much are these trousers?
Assistant They're £17.50.
Customer Have you got them in a size 32?
Assistant Just a minute. Yes, here you are. Size 32.
Customer Thank you. Can I try them on?
Assistant Yes, of course. The changing rooms are over there.
Customer Thank you.

Later
Assistant How are they?
Customer They're fine, thanks. I'll take them.
Assistant Do you want anything else?
Customer No, thanks.
Assistant That's £47.50 then, please.
Customer Here you are.
Assistant Thank you. That's £2.50 change.
Customer Thank you. Goodbye.
Assistant Goodbye.

2 **Assistant** Can I help you?
Customer Yes. How much are these trainers, please?
Assistant They're £84.99.
Customer Have you got them in a size 10?
Assistant Just a minute. Yes, here you are. Size 10.
Customer Thank you. I'll just try them on.
Later
Assistant How are they?
Customer They're fine, thanks. I'll take them.
Assistant Do you want anything else?
Customer Yes. Could I have these socks, please?
Assistant That's £99.98 altogether then, please.
Customer Can I pay by credit card?
Assistant Yes of course. Could you sign here, please? Thank you. There you are.
Customer Thank you. Goodbye.
Assistant Bye.

3 **Assistant** Can I help you?
Customer Yes. How much is this tracksuit?
Assistant It's £63.20.

Customer Have you got it in a medium size?
Assistant Yes, here you are. Medium.
Customer Thank you. Where can I try it on?
Assistant The changing rooms are over there, next to the jeans.
Customer Thank you.

Later
Assistant How is it?
Customer It's fine, thanks. I'll take it.
Assistant Do you want anything else?
Customer Yes, can I have this cap?
Assistant That's £68.70 then, please.
Customer Do you take credit cards?
Assistant Certainly. Could you sign here, please? There you are. That's your copy.
Customer Thank you. Goodbye.
Assistant Goodbye.

12.1

Interviewer Why did you decide to go to a health farm?
Guest I was fatter and heavier than I wanted to be.
Interviewer Why did you choose Henley Manor? Was it cheaper than other places?
Guest No, in fact it was more expensive than some other places, but it was nearer home, so it was more convenient.
Interviewer What was it like?
Guest Well, it was more difficult than I expected. In fact after two days I felt worse than before, but after that things became easier.
Interviewer And how do you feel now?
Guest I feel a lot happier. I'm slimmer and I feel ten years younger! I eat healthier food now, and my lifestyle is slower and more relaxed. I go to bed earlier and I sleep better.

12.2

1 **A** What's the matter?
B I'm tired.
A Well, you shouldn't stay up so late.
B I know, but there was a good film on the telly last night.
2 **A** What's wrong?
B I'm hungry.
A You should have something to eat, then.
B But there's nothing in the fridge.
3 **A** Are you all right?
B No, I'm not. I've got toothache.
A Well, you should go to the dentist's.
B Yes, you're right.
4 **A** What's up?
B My back hurts.
A Well, you should go and see the doctor.
B No, it's not that bad.
5 **A** What's the matter?
B I can't read that sign.
A Well, you should go to the optician's and get some glasses.
B Hmm. Perhaps you're right.
6 **A** What's wrong?
B I've got stomach ache.
A Well, you shouldn't eat so much.
B Yes, I know.
7 **A** What's up?
B I'm cold.
A You should put a jumper on, then.
B Well, why don't we go inside?
8 **A** Are you all right?
B No, I don't feel well. I think I've got a cold.
A Well, you shouldn't go out this evening, then. You should go to bed.
B But it's Zara's party this evening.

Extension Units 11 and 12

1 **A** Were you here last week, Maria?
B No, I wasn't. I didn't feel very well.
A Oh, I'm sorry to hear that. What was wrong?
B I had a sore throat and a headache.
A Did you go to the doctor's?
B No, I didn't. I just stayed in bed.
A Do you feel better now?
B Yes, I'm fine now, thanks.
2 **A** Were you away yesterday, Pedro?
B Yes, I was at the hospital.
A Why? What was up?
B I fell downstairs and hurt my wrist.
A Oh dear! Is it all right?
B Yes, it isn't broken.
A That's good. Does it still hurt?
B Well it's better today, but it hurts when I move it.
3 **A** Where were you yesterday, Anne?
B I was at the dentist's. I had terrible toothache.
A Oh dear. That doesn't sound very nice.
B No, it wasn't. It really hurt. I couldn't sleep on Sunday night.
A Is it better now?
B Oh yes, it's fine.
4 **A** Were you away last week, Sanjit?
B Yes, I was. I was ill.
A Oh, what was the matter?
B I had a very bad cold.
A Did you go to the doctor's?
B Yes, I did, and he gave me some medicine.
A How's your cold now?
B Well, I've still got a cough, but it was a lot worse last week.

Extension Units 11 and 12
Great balls of fire

You shake my nerves and you rattle my brain,
Too much love drives a man insane.
You broke my will,
But what a thrill.
Goodness gracious! Great balls of fire.
I laughed at love 'cos I thought it was funny,
You came along and moved me, honey,
I've changed my mind,
This world is fine.
Goodness gracious! Great balls of fire.
Mmm, kiss me, baby.
Ooh, it feels good.
Hold me, baby.
I want to love you like a lover should.
You're fine,
So kind.
I want to tell the world you're mine, mine, mine, mine.
I chew my nails and I twiddle my thumbs,
I'm real nervous but it sure is fun.
Come on, baby,
Drive me crazy.
Goodness gracious! Great balls of fire.

13.1

DJ Hello. I'm at the *Top Band Show* here in London. An hour ago Flight won the prize for 'Best New Band of the Year'. I'm going to talk to their singer, Kate Mahoney. First, congratulations, Kate! Tell us about the prize.
Kate Well, the most important thing is that we're going to go on tour with some really famous bands next year. That's going to be great!
DJ And are you going to make an album?
Kate We don't know yet. Our manager's going to see some record companies next week.

Tapescripts

DJ Now, you also won £5,000. How are you going to spend it?

Kate We're going to buy new equipment for the band.

DJ Good idea. What about a holiday?

Kate No, we aren't going to take a holiday – we haven't got time!

DJ Is this prize going to help you?

Kate Yes, it is, but it isn't going to change things overnight. We're going to have to work hard to make it to the top.

DJ Now, your bass guitarist, Ryan Sweet, is still at university. Is he going to join you on tour?

Kate No, he isn't. He isn't going to stay in the band – he's going to finish his studies at university.

DJ Are you going to look for a new bass player?

Kate Yes, we are. So if you can play the bass guitar, we want to hear from you!

DJ OK, Kate. Thanks very much. Now Jack Dee's going to tell us something about the other bands.

🔊 13.2

1 A Shall we go out for a meal on Saturday night?

B Mmm, that would be nice.

A Where would you like to go?

B How about that new Japanese restaurant in the square?

A Good idea. Is eight o'clock all right?

B Yes, eight's fine.

A Right. Shall I give the restaurant a ring and make a reservation?

B OK. Here's the phone book.

2 A Why don't we go out somewhere this afternoon?

B OK.

A What shall we do?

B Erm. Let's go bowling.

A Good idea. What time do you want to go?

B Oh, not too early. I can call for you at 2.30.

A No. Let's meet at the bowling alley, because I'm going to be in town this morning.

B Well, would you like to meet for lunch, then?

A OK. We can get lunch at the bowling alley.

B Right. See you there then. Is half past one OK?

A Fine. See you then.

3 A Would you like to go away for the weekend?

B Mmm, that would be great.

A Where shall we go?

B How about Paris?

A Oh, yes! Shall we go on Friday evening or Saturday morning?

B Let's go on Friday. Then we can have longer there.

A OK. I'm going to be near the travel agent's in the morning, so I can call in and book something.

B Great.

4 A Why don't we go out tonight?

B Good idea.

A Where shall we go?

B There's a good film on at the cinema.

A OK. What time does it start?

B I don't know.

A Just a minute. Let's have a look in the local paper. Er, the last performance is at 7.45.

B That's in an hour's time.

A OK. Let's go and get ready then.

🔊 13.5

1 What's he going to do?
2 Would you like to go bowling?
3 I'm going to sing a song.
4 I want to be at the meeting.
5 What's her husband like?
6 What are you doing?
7 What sports does she like?
8 We missed the train yesterday.
9 Where's he going to live?
10 I don't want to get up.

🔊 14.2

Part 1

Mandy Hello?

Russell Hello. Is that Mandy Poole?

Mandy Yes, it is.

Russell This is Russell Dean. You're on *Lucky Break*.

Mandy What? Oh, I don't believe it!

Russell Well, it's true. Have you ever been on TV before?

Mandy No, I haven't.

Russell Well, Mandy, you are now. Do you watch the show every day?

Mandy Yes, I do.

Russell Where do you live?

Mandy I live in London.

Russell What do you do?

Mandy I'm a teacher.

Russell Are you married?

Mandy Yes, I am.

Russell What's your husband's name?

Mandy His name's Peter.

Russell What does he do?

Mandy He works in an office.

Russell Is he listening at the moment?

Mandy No, he isn't. He's having a shower.

Russell Is he going to miss you on TV?

Mandy Yes, he is.

Russell Well, now, today's prize is a weekend for two in New York. I'm going to ask you four questions.

Part 2

Russell I'm going to ask you four questions. Are you ready?

Mandy Yes, I am.

Russell OK. Here are the questions. One: Is China larger than Russia or smaller than Russia?

Mandy It's smaller.

Russell Correct. Two: What are the most dangerous animals in the world? Sharks, rats, or snakes?

Mandy Oh, er, rats.

Russell Correct. Rats kill more people than sharks or snakes. Question three: Where is the tallest tree in the world? Is it in Australia, Scotland, or California?

Mandy I think it's in California, isn't it?

Russell Yes, you're right. It's an incredible 111 metres tall. Now the last question. Where is the hottest place in the world? Is it in the United States, in India, or in Africa? Think carefully now. The United States, India, or Africa?

Mandy Oh, erm, I'll say Africa.

Russell Yes! It's a place called Dallol in Africa. Well done!

Mandy Oh, I can't believe it!

Russell Yes! You've won today's prize. You and your husband, Peter, are going to spend a wonderful weekend in New York. Congratulations!

Irregular verbs

Infinitive	Past tense	Past participle
be	was / were	been
become	became	become
begin	began	begun
break	broke	broken
bring	brought	brought
build	built	built
buy	bought	bought
catch	caught	caught
choose	chose	chosen
come	came	come
cost	cost	cost
cut	cut	cut
do	did	done
draw	drew	drawn
drink	drank	drunk
drive	drove	driven
eat	ate	eaten
fall	fell	fallen
feel	felt	felt
find	found	found
fly	flew	flown
forget	forgot	forgotten
get	got	got
give	gave	given
go	went	gone
have	had	had
hear	heard	heard
hit	hit	hit
hold	held	held
hurt	hurt	hurt
keep	kept	kept
know	knew	known
leave	left	left
lose	lost	lost
make	made	made
meet	met	met
pay	paid	paid
put	put	put
read	read	read
ride	rode	ridden
ring	rang	rung
run	ran	run
say	said	said
see	saw	seen
sell	sold	sold
send	sent	sent
shine	shone	shone
sing	sang	sung
sit	sat	sat
sleep	slept	slept
speak	spoke	spoken
spend	spent	spent
stand	stood	stood
swim	swam	swum
take	took	taken
teach	taught	taught
tell	told	told
think	thought	thought
understand	understood	understood
wake up	woke up	woken up
wear	wore	worn
win	won	won
write	wrote	written

International Phonetic Alphabet (IPA)

Vowels and diphthongs

/iː/	see	/siː/
/i/	happy	/'hæpi/
/ɪ/	sit	/sɪt/
/e/	ten	/ten/
/æ/	hat	/hæt/
/ɑː/	arm	/ɑːm/
/ɒ/	got	/gɒt/
/ɔː/	saw	/sɔː/
/ʊ/	put	/pʊt/
/uː/	too	/tuː/
/ʌ/	cup	/kʌp/
/ɜː/	fur	/fɜː(r)/
/ə/	ago	/ə'gəʊ/
/eɪ/	page	/peɪʤ/
/əʊ/	home	/həʊm/
/aɪ/	five	/faɪv/
/aʊ/	now	/naʊ/
/ɔɪ/	join	/ʤɔɪn/
/ɪə/	near	/nɪə(r)/
/eə/	hair	/heə/
/ʊə/	pure	/pjʊə(r)/

Consonants

/p/	pen	/pen/
/b/	bad	/bæd/
/t/	tea	/tiː/
/d/	did	/dɪd/
/k/	cat	/kæt/
/g/	got	/gɒt/
/ʧ/	chin	/ʧɪn/
/ʤ/	June	/ʤuːn/
/l/	fall	/fɔːl/
/v/	voice	/vɔɪs/
/θ/	thin	/θɪn/
/ð/	then	/ðen/
/s/	so	/səʊ/
/z/	zoo	/zuː/
/ʃ/	she	/ʃiː/
/ʒ/	vision	/'vɪʒn/
/h/	how	/haʊ/
/m/	man	/mæn/
/n/	no	/nəʊ/
/ŋ/	sing	/sɪŋ/
/l/	leg	/leg/
/r/	red	/red/
/j/	yes	/jes/
/w/	wet	/wet/

Acknowledgements

The author would especially like to record his gratitude to his wife, Eunice, and his children, without whose support and patience *Lifelines* would not have been written.

The author would also like to thank all those at Oxford University Press who have contributed their skills and ideas to producing this course.

The publishers and author are very grateful to all the teachers and institutions involved in reading and/or piloting *Lifelines* for providing invaluable comment and feedback on the course. We would especially like to thank: Derek Acland, Eszter Baumann, and Laurence Kinsella (International House, Budapest, Hungary), Fergus Auld and Siobhan Blaschek (English in York, York, UK), Richard Baudains, Anne Murray, and Christabel Powell (British School, Trieste, Italy), Éva Berényi, Katalin Izsák, and Rhiannon Williams (Coventry House, Kecskemét, Hungary), Catherine Bond (Oxford English Centre, Oxford, UK), Eleanor Cave (Torbay Language Centre, Paignton, UK), Daniel Chavant, Isabelle Massard, and Catriona Osborne (CCI Eure et Loir, Chartres, France), A. Cosgrove (English Language Institute, Dublin, Ireland), Alison Edge (British Council, Bilbao, Spain), Alexandra Gibson and Sarah Stratford (British Council, Bologna, Italy), Barbara Mackay (freelance, UK), Filipa Plant dos Santos (Inlingua, Porto, Portugal), Mike Sayer (Regent Oxford, Oxford, UK), Hanna Sciepurko (British Council Studium, Gdańsk, Poland), Russell Stannard (CLIC IH, Seville, Spain), Joanna Thompson (Devon School of English, Paignton, UK), Fiona Williamson (Oxford Academy, Oxford, UK)

Illustrations by:
Kathy Baxendale p 68; Adrian Barclay pp 27 (icons), 35, 36, 37, 49 (prepositions), 59, 65; Mike Bell p 64; Rowie Christopher p 54; Mark Draisey pp 8, 14, 18, 27, 42, 64, 77, 78, 97, 112, 113, 114; Tim Kahane pp 28, 32, 45, 47; Mac Macintosh p 50; Stephen May pp 16, 21, 22, 84, 85, 90, 91; Ian Mitchell pp 9, 10, 11, 55, 70, 71, 88, 89, 98; Anthony Rule pp 6, 24, 25, 69, 86, 87; Technical Graphics Dept, OUP pp 68, 70; Mark Thomas pp 48, 49, 60, 61

Location photography by:
Gareth Boden pp 6, 12, 13, 15, 19, 26, 34, 38, 41, 44 (fruit shop), 47, 51 (students), 52 (symbols, postbox), 62, 72, 76, 79, 80, 91, 96, 100

Studio photography by:
Mark Mason pp 23, 29 (papers), 30, 52 (keyring), 56

The publishers would like to thank the following for their permission to reproduce photographs:
J Allen Cash Photolibrary pp 7 (Married Black Couple), 43 (Skiers – Arosa), 44 (Midland Bank), 96 (Helicopter); Allsport UK Ltd p 93 (Tiger Woods); Alpha p 71 (K Tsuchida); Aquarius Picture Library p 103 (Spencer: For Hire); Arcaid p 51 (Early 20th C. Housing/ Viv Porter); Bubbles Photolibrary p 7 (Men/P Sylent); Earthwatch Europe p 9 (Marine Mammalogy/B McNulty, Forests of Bohemia/ M O'Neill); Greg Evans International pp 7 (Ethnic Girl 17 yrs), 42 (Chalet Girl), 51 (House Boat), 52 (Campsite); Eye Ubiquitous p 94 (the Empire Cinema); Famous Pictures and Features Agency p 103 (Di Marco Family – Eastenders/J Miles, M Collins/P Aitchison); Getty Images cover (Crowd), pp 30 (Female Exec. on Phone/ P Correz), 37 (Couple Running/J Polollio), 44 (Pupils Leaving School/B Bidwell); the Golf Picture Library p 93 (Tiger Woods Smiling/M Harris, Tiger Woods/M Harris); David and Emma Illsley p 56 (Cyclists); the Imagebank pp 7 (Asian Woman/S Marks, Young Hispanic Man/N Russell), 11 (Diner/J Cadge), 29 (W/Cake – Montage/A Duey, Flag by Ballot Box/ITTC Productions), 94 (Ten Pin Bowling/P McConville), 96 (Indy Car Racing/W Sallaz); Sally Lack p 63 (Young Woman); Jerry Lambert pp 33, 61, 89 (Clouds); Milepost 92.5 p 40 (Euro Train); Oxford Scientific Films p 99 (Trochilidae Flower/M Fogden, Radio-tracking/M Coe); George Phillips Associates p 66 (E Halliday); Pictor International pp 33 (Lady on Telephone), 37 (Elderly Couple by Tractor), 44 (Science Museum, Paddington Station), 51 (Farmhouse), 52 (Century City), 82 (Massage), 94 (Theatre, Disco, the White Horse Pub, New York City), 96 (Diving, Riding, Gliding); Popperfoto p 62 (A Morsov); Power Stock/Zefa p 20 (Couple Outdoors); Quadrant Picture Library p 29 (Vauxhall Corsa, Iveco Ford Lorry, Harley Davidson, Motorbike – Tunisia/Tony Hobbs); Redferns p 58 (A Ssempeke/ H Butler, Glastonbury Festival/N Hutson, Womad Festival/ D Peabody); Rex Features pp 44 (Tesco 24hr Shopping/A Testa), 79 (Model on Catwalk); South West News Service p 66 (Riverside/ Sainsbury's); the Stock Market/Zefa pp 33 (Young Man on Telephone), 82 (Exercise Class); Tony Stone Images pp 52

(Shopping Centre/S Johnson), 68 (Inca Ruins/M Scott), 82 (Woman Eating Salad/D Day); Telegraph Colour Library pp 7 (Middle Aged/Retired couple/J Lawler), 15 (Couple Walking on Beach), 20 (Man & 2 Women at Table/B Ling, Expectant Couple/ J Cummins, 3 Men & 2 Women in Café/Bluestone Productions), 29 (Full Ashtray/Werner Otto, Glass of Beer/Bildagentur, Roulette Wheel/B&M Productions), 40 (Man Working From Home/P Hunt), 75 (Pancorbo – North Spain), 94 (Japanese & European Diners/ S Benbow); John Walmsley pp 9 (Young Woman), 83 (Woman Laughing)

Songs:
Great Balls of Fire Words and music by Jack Hammer and Otis Blackwell, © 1957 Hill & Range Songs, Inc administered throughout the world by Unichappell Inc, lyric reproduction by kind permission of Carlin Music Corp, Iron Bridge House, 3 Bridge Approach, Chalk Farm, London, NE1 8BD

Wild Thing Words and music by Chip Taylor, © 1966 EMI Blackwood Music Inc, USA, EMI Music Publishing Ltd, London, WC2H 0EA, reproduced by permission of IMP Ltd

You've got to hide your love away Lyrics by John Lennon and Paul McCartney, taken from the song *You've got to hide your love away* by kind permission Sony/ATV Music Publishing Ltd

The publishers are grateful to those who have given permission to reproduce the following extracts and adaptations of copyright material:
p66 'Move out for £250,000 and a cruise? No, said Miss Eileen, I stay put' © Daily Mail/Solo Syndication
p70 'Torquay? I thought I was going to Turkey' by Christopher Evans © Daily Mail/Solo Syndication

The publishers would like to thank the following for their time and assistance:
Alders (Oxford), the Angel & Greyhound Pub, the Ark (Frilford), Beans (Bicester), Carlton TV, Four Pillars Hotels, George & Davis, the Masons Pub, Margarita North (British Council, Lima, Perú), Oxygen Radio, Police Constable Martin Robinson (Education Liaison Officer, Lancashire Constabulary), Shepherd & Woodward, Tesco, Thomas Cook (Oxford), Top Fruits

Oxford University Press
Great Clarendon Street
Oxford OX2 6DP

Oxford   New York
Athens   Auckland   Bangkok   Bogotá
Buenos Aires   Calcutta   Cape Town   Chennai
Dar es Salaam   Delhi   Florence   Hong Kong
Istanbul   Karachi   Kuala Lumpur   Madrid
Melbourne   Mexico City   Mumbai   Nairobi
Paris   São Paulo   Singapore   Taipei   Tokyo
Toronto   Warsaw

and associated companies in
Berlin   Ibadan

OXFORD and OXFORD ENGLISH
are trade marks of Oxford University Press

ISBN 0 19 433874 6

© Oxford University Press 1999

First published 1999
Fifth impression 2000
5 4 3 2 1

No unauthorized photocopying

Designed by Holdsworth Associates, Isle of Wight

Printed in Dubai